THE NEW COMPLETE
AKITA

TACHIBANA-GO
This Akita bitch was the model for the Japanese 2-Yen stamp.

THE NEW COMPLETE
AKITA

Joan M. Linderman

AND

Virginia B. Funk

HOWELL
BOOK HOUSE
New York

Macmillan General Reference
A Simon & Schuster Macmillan Company
1633 Broadway
New York, NY 10019-6785

MACMILLAN is a registered trademark of Macmillan, Inc.

Library of Congress Cataloging-in-Publication Data

Linderman, Joan M.
    The new complete Akita / Joan M. Linderman and Virginia Funk.
        p.   cm.
    Includes bibliographical references (p.   ).
    ISBN 0-87605-031-3
    1. Akita Dogs.   I. Funk, Virginia.   II. Title.   III. Title:
Akita.
SF429.A65L565   1994
636.7'3—dc20   94-15210
                                                                           CIP

Manufactured in the United States of America

10 9 8 7 6 5 4 3 2

We dedicate this book to a close friend, Anne Diener, and all of the other Akita fanciers who are no longer at ringside with us.

Anne Diener with Champion Sakusaku's Diamond Lil.

Acknowledgments

A SPECIAL THANK YOU to Donald Lusk, a student of the breed, for the chapter on the Akita in Japan.

To Sheryl Langan for her contribution of the breed history and pictures of Akitas in Canada.

To Dr. Shinichi Ishiguro, Dr. Keiichi Ogasawara, Mrs. S. Ichikawa, Mrs. Taro Matsudo, Richard Kawamoto, Dr. Tatsuo Kimura and Dr. Joseph Vogl, just a few of the devoted admirers of the Akita breed, and friends who have contributed pictures and background history.

To Eric Linderman, Dr. Shinichi Ishiguro and C. Kam for illustrations.

To Bill Bobrow and Sandy Batausa for their writings.

To all the people who have supplied photos and information but are too many to list individually, a gracious thank you. Most of your names and/or pictures appear elsewhere in the text.

And last, but not by any means least, our appreciation to the Akita Club of America and its 1993 president, Camille C. Kam, and the Akitainu Hozonkai, Los Angeles, Branch and its 1993 president, George Hamano, for their cooperation.

Contents

Acknowledgments **vii**

Foreword
by Joan Linderman **xv**

Prologue
by Donald W. Lusk **xvii**

1. The Early History of the Akita in Japan
   by Donald W. Lusk **1**
   The Akita Is Brought to America   *7*

2. Great Dogs of Japan and Their Influence on the Breed **13**
   Faithful Hachiko   *33*

3. The Akita in America **41**
   Early Contributions and the Road to American Kennel
     Club Recognition   *41*
   Early Breed Clubs and Their Impact on the Breed   *42*
   The Miscellaneous Class at AKC Shows   *43*
   The Road to Recognition   *44*

4. Akitas in America—Past and Present   **49**

The Early Days   *49*
East Coast Foundations   *57*
The Beginning of One American Kennel *as told by Sandy*
    Batausa   60
The Outlook   *71*

5. The Evolution of the Parent Club Standard   **73**

Japanese Standards   *74*
    The Standard Points of the ''Nippon-Inu''   74
    Standards for the Japanese Large Size Breed   76
    Akitainu Standard   81
An Analysis of the Akitainu Hozonkai Standard
    for the Akita   *83*
The Present Breed Standard   *93*
In Conclusion   *97*

6. An Analysis of the Akita—As It Stands   **99**

Proportion   *99*
Head   *99*
Ears   *100*
Eyes   *100*
Mouth   *100*
Neck   *100*
Body   *100*
Tail   *101*
Anus   *101*
Legs and Feet   *101*
Comment   *101*
Summary   *101*

7. The Importance of Color   **107**

What Impact Does Color Have in the Show Ring?   *107*
The AKC Standard on Color   *108*
In Conclusion   *110*

8. The Adaptability of the Akita   **111**

Obedience   *112*
    In the Beginning   112

  Obedience and the Akita by Bill Bobrow   *114*
    Two Firsts—Ch. Sukoshi Kuma, CDX   *126*
  Power Pulling   *126*
  Dog Sledding   *127*
  Schutzhund   *128*
  The Akita as a Hunter   *129*

9. "Dottie"—The Story of an Akita Guide Dog
    by Bill Bobrow   **135**
  An Akita as a Guide Dog?   *137*
  Pilot Dogs   *138*
  Will She Qualify?   *139*
  Dottie's Training   *140*
  The Evaluation   *143*
  A New Beginning   *145*
  Epilogue *by Virginia Funk*   *146*

10. Breeding and Whelping   **147**
  Ready—or Not?   *148*
  The Breeding   *149*
  The Pregnancy   *150*
  Supplies   *151*
    The Whelping Box   *151*
    The Outside Pen   *152*
    The First-Aid Kit   *152*
  The Whelping   *154*
  Conclusion   *158*

11. Your New Akita Litter—After the Whelping   **159**
  There Are Pitfalls   *160*
    Danger Signals   *162*
  Weaning   *162*
  Record Keeping   *165*
  Worming and Care   *166*
  Culling   *167*
  Registering and Selling the Puppies   *169*

12. Specialty Clubs in the United States   **173**
  The Akita Club of America   *173*

Regions   174
Member Clubs   174
Club Biographies   176
   Squakheag Akita Club   176
   Rocky Mountain Akita Club, Inc.   176
Akitainu Hozonkai   *178*

13.   Evolution of the Breed in Canada   **181**

The Canadian Parent Club   *182*
Early Firsts   *187*
The Canadian Breed Standard   *187*
A Special Dog in Canada   *193*
   Neh-Wa's Story   193

14.   Specialty Shows and Events—Before
        and After AKC Recognition   **199**

The First Specialty Shows   *200*
Specialties Since AKC Recognition   *208*
Specialty Contributions   *214*

15.   The Show Ring in Japan and America   **219**

Japan   *219*
   Presentation   220
   Procedure and Protocol   221
   The Japan Kennel Club   225
In America   *225*
   How Dogs Are Judged   227
   The Point System   228
      Regular Classes   228
      Winners   230
A First—and a Path to the Future   *231*
   Brownie's Story   231

16.   The Register of Merit   **233**

ROM Sires   *234*
ROM Dams   *240*

In Conclusion   **251**

Glossary of Terms   **253**

Bibliography of Akita-Related Sources   **257**

About the Authors   **259**

Foreword

Welcome to the Akita.

For several decades, the beloved dogs that have shared my house have been the exotic Japanese breed known as Akitas.

Having become a student of the breed over the past thirty years, it is a pleasure to share some of this information with others.

As you study the pictures throughout the text you will see a transformation to a more visually sophisticated breed, alike in type and with a vibrancy of color, has evolved in Japan. If you look even more closely, you will see that the same pattern is taking place in the United States.

The Akita is an exciting breed, and Virginia and I fervently hope that you will enjoy this book as much as we have enjoyed constructing it for you.

—Joan Linderman

Prologue

Donald Lusk has been involved with the Akita breed for nearly twenty-five years; initially as a breeder-exhibitor, but more particularly as a student of the breed.

During the mid-1970s and early 1980s, Don and Twyla Lusk made several trips to Japan doing research and gathering material for their award-winning publication, *The Akita Journal*.

Don has served as president of the Akita Club of America and has been active in many Akita Specialty and all-breed organizations, including the Dog Writers Association of America.

For well over twenty years I have sought to piece together a coherent history of the Akita, the origins, evolution and rightful place of this breed in the social and cultural mosaic of Japan and America. However, the tapestry I have attempted to weave more resembles a patchwork: fragmented, speculative and incomplete at best.

The more I have probed into Akita lore, the more difficult it has become to separate fact from myth, informed opinion from gross speculation. The contemporary history of the Akita, in both written and photographic form, has been chronicled by numerous Japanese and American authors reaching significantly different conclusions about how the Akita's history has evolved.

In the case of American authors, too often their conclusions have been based on what they have heard or read from other sources and not from inquiry or personal observation. As for Japanese Akita historians, to some degree their opionions are colored by their own preconceptions, the particular segment of Akita infrastructure they represent, and, as is so prevalent in the sub-culture of dog breeding and exhibiting everywhere in the world, their personal goals, biases and considerations.

These differing views have been exacerbated by various international events during the first fifty years of the twentieth century, which catapulted Japan from an insular near-feudal state to a position of economic, political and military power. The years immediately preceding, during and following World War II had an incalculable impact on Japan's sense of its own history, and its relationship with everything "American." I believe that the direction of Akita breeding in post–World War II Japan was profoundly influenced by Japan's yearning to repair its shattered self-image and restore dignity to its cultural heritage. As recorded by Japanese authors during that period, Akita history could not escape being influenced by these sweeping social and cultural issues and trends.

During five visits to Japan from the mid-1970s through the early 1980s, my wife, Twyla, and I had the opportunity to examine hundreds of Akitas on Honshu. Our quest for visual exposure to Akitas ran the gamut: Akitas in the regional and AKIHO headquarters shows; Akitas in major urban centers, such as Tokyo, Yokohama, Osaka, Nara, Fukuoka and Hiroshima; Akitas in the small villages and hamlets of the northern Tohoku district and, particularly, Akita prefecture at the northern extremity of the big island; Akitas in Odate, the historical and cultural mecca of the breed; Akitas on the streets; Akitas as pets; Akitas insensitively chained and caged at commercial dog dealers.

During those forays, it was our good fortune to meet, interview and befriend some of the true patrons and scholars of the Akita breed. Our many hours with Heihachi Hashimoto, owner of Kongo-go, were, in retrospect, priceless moments. Our experience has also been nurtured and enriched by the many days we spent traveling and talking with the likes of Dr. Ogasawara, Naoto Kajiwara, Dr. Ishiguro and others, as well as long hours spent examining historical artifacts, photographs and skeletal remains of great Akitas at the AKIHO headquarters museum in Odate.

Reviewing my notes, tapes and manuscripts originated during and immediately following those years of intense inquiry of Japan, it is clear that I accepted most of what I heard or read as unvarnished historical fact. In retrospect, I can only now begin to recognize the subtle nuance of "personal points-of-view" which were co-mingled with representations of historical fact.

Our interviews in 1978 with Heihachi Hashimoto in Tokyo offered a rare glimpse of a man within whose bosom still smoldered the competitive embers ignited by his famous Akita Kongo-go more than three decades before. The success of Kongo in the show ring and as a stud dog brought Hashimoto fame and great financial reward. Kongo changed Hashimoto's life from what it would have been. Should it then come as any surprise that the owners and breeders of the equally revered Goramaru-go would have a significantly different account from Hashimoto's of the ultimate face-off between these two great dogs in the show ring?

We have also been blessed with the opportunity of working in America with our friend Dr. Tats Kimura, who has so meticulously translated many Akita texts and manuscripts into English over the past twenty years—and of course, the years of friendship with Niki Rhoden, who is in our view the premier Akita scholar in America.

One might then conclude, and I might mistakenly represent, that this great window of exposure and experience I have enjoyed qualifies me as an authority on Akita history. Quite the opposite is true. I am increasingly quick to challenge simplistic conclusions to complex questions. This still makes a clear understanding of Akita history difficult. For example, even early confirmation of the breed is shrouded in mystery. I have yet to discover any irrefutable evidence that the Akita dog, as it exists either in Japan or America today, is by type, size, structure, conformation and temperament the same dog which existed in Japanese antiquity.

Sometimes the study of a breed is greatly enhanced by artistic renderings of the breed throughout its evolution. That usually reliable reference tool is absent in the historical study of the Akita. In the case of art in Japan, one cannot be sure of the fidelity of artistic representation. The following excerpt from *The Hokusai Sketch Books* by James Michener describes this phenomenon:

> Certain of the pages also illustrate one of the most perplexing, if completely trivial problems of Japanese art, yet in its contemplation, one comes to grips with an artistic problem of first-rate magnitude. Hokusai, like all Japanese artists, was quite incompetent in drawing dogs or puppies. Some of the most improbable monstrosities cluttering the pages of Japanese art purport to represent dogs; they are formless, misshapen and characterless. If one artist alone, or one school or one generation exhibited this deficiency, it could be dismissed as a chance aberration, but when all do, it becomes a problem of genetic art. The explanation seems simple. The earliest Japanese artists got off on the wrong foot, saw dogs improperly, depicted them so, and no successor ever got the matter straightened out.

In a landmark article, "Myths and Legends of the Dog in Ancient Japan" (*Akita Journal,* 1980), Niki Rhoden addresses another aspect of Japanese literature, which precludes accepting Japanese dog history as a literal chronology.

> The historical literature of old Japan is a fascinating mixture of truth and yarn. Scholars of Japanese history have burned many a midnight candle trying to decipher the often complex modes of narration. In studying each work as a tapestry, their task has been to separate the warp from the weft, for not only are the threads an interweaving of pomp, proclamation and politics, but richly colored with martial exploits and spiritual wisdom and couched in superstition and occult art. The mores of the day, of course, were reflections of religious teaching and sovereign decree, but such teachings and decrees sometimes were expressed through fanciful tales. The substance of many early manuscripts is now known to be mostly mythical concoction, but the themes make delightful reading even for sophisticates, and the stories involving dogs are particularly captivating to lovers of the Japanese dog.

There is considerable scientific data relative to the form of Japanese dogs as they existed in the early 1800s. However, the best source of this research is Western Europe, not Japan. Dr. Phillip Von Seibold, a German physician and naturalist living in Japan from 1823 until 1829, brought a Japanese dog back to the Netherlands. This animal is now preserved and displayed at Leiden's Museum of Natural History. Von Seibold also drew numerous illustrations accompanied by detailed description of dogs he encountered in Japan. The following excerpt from an article about Von Seibold by Hiroma Koga (published in *Aiken No Tomo,* September 1989), was written following his review of Von Seibold's work during a visit to Leiden.

> Among the paragraphs on mammals appear illustrations of dogs. This is limited to only a page. However, to those of us who are researchers of Japanese dogs, those illustrations are priceless data. Von Seibold has a general classification of three kinds of Japanese dogs: the hunting dog, the city dog and the indoor dog (Japanese spaniel). The hunting dog and the city dog are illustrated, but a drawing of a side view of the hunting dog is especially superb. Needless to say, that among the drawings by Japanese artists of the Edo period (1615–1868), there is not one among them that is as accurate and realistic as these illustrations. As I ponder over this, Dutch art has a tradition of realism that goes back 300 to 400 years before the time of Seibold and Rembrandt.

I have seen copies of the Von Seibold drawing of the Japanese hunting dog, which Koga describes as follows: "shallow stop, triangular, sharp eyes, flat, broad forehead, front pasterns having sufficient angulation, hocks are deep, the abdomen is tucked up, dark red coat, standing tail, deep chest."

Assuming from the foregoing that Von Seibold's illustrations are much closer to historical reality than those images depicted by Japanese artists, the form of these early dogs (which obviously were part of the biological ancestry of today's Akita) is nearly unrecognizable in the form of the Akita as we now know it. This is stunning when one considers this to be only about 150 years ago.

Michael Kammen, in his recent book *Mystic Chords of Memory,* puts an interesting spin on the interplay of history and mythology:

> Historiographers (historians of history) are coming round to the view that history consists of little more than a series of consensual myths. It is not a nation's past that shapes its mythology, but a nation's mythology that determines its past. History becomes a minstrel show, glimpsed through a musty lens, distorted by tradition, popular culture and wishful thinking.

It is not my intent to depreciate the value of any previous contributions to our knowledge of Akita history, nor to diminish our appreciation of those many sincere individuals in Japan and America who have searched for the truth about this magnificent yet mysterious breed. My hope is that we continue our search for a better understanding of the *real* history of this breed; that we not be content to repeat hearsay and fiction and that we diligently and objectively pursue true knowledge of the Akita.

A fitting conclusion to this prologue to Akita history are these words from *When Artists Distort History*, an essay by Lance Morrow: "Better to opt for information and conjecture and the exhumation of all theories. Let a hundred flowers bloom, even if some of them are poisonous and paranoid. A culture is what it remembers and knows."

—Donald W. Lusk

THE NEW COMPLETE
AKITA

1 大型種（秋田犬） 2 中型種（猪犬） 3 小型種（芝犬） 4 土佐犬 5 狆
AKITA　　　INOSHISHI　　SHIBA　TOSA　CHIN

Copy of a painting done by N. Higashi in 1933 in Japan.

1

The Early History of the Akita in Japan

by Donald W. Lusk

WHEN JOAN ASKED ME to revise the chapter I wrote for *The Complete Akita* in 1983 she probably assumed that my knowledge of that era of Akita history had grown in depth and breadth during the intervening decade.

I find that there has not been appreciable growth in the body of fact and evidence available to us, but instead a blurring of conventional wisdom on which we tend to rely. That is the reason for my preceding Prologue to Akita history, by which I attempt to put this or any other Akita history into perspective.

The first obstacle in constructing this history is the limited research and written material available. Second is the inevitable difficulty in securing accurate translations of such material from the original Japanese. Third, there is a diversity of opinion even among the handful of scholars who have made a serious effort to search out and chronicle the facts.

Though Japan offers us over 2,600 years of recorded history

and civilization, the fragments of that long and colorful history that shed any conclusive light on the true origins of the Akita dog, as we know it today, are sparse indeed.

There are but a handful of Japanese scientific and lay authors who over the past century have devoted significant effort to sorting out the origins and development of the Japanese type dog in general, and the Akita in particular. Their conclusions and speculations are based on archaeological, cultural, zoological, anthropological and ethnological viewpoints. Also important are those whose studies have been primarily pursued through review of what written history has been documented by folklore and those closely identified with "Japanese dog culture."

One of the most disciplined investigations of the origin of the Akita is currently being conducted by Niki Rhoden of Oakland, California. Hers is the only research I am aware of based on the pure biological aspects of the Akita. Her findings, if published, may prove to be highly surprising and certainly more scientifically conclusive than most.

Some of the more accepted and respected authorities on the subject in Japan include: Dr. Toku Uchida, author of *Inu No Hon (Book on Dogs)*; Dr. Shosaburo Watase; Mr. Hirokichi Saito, founder of Nihon-Ken, and author of *Nihon No Inu To Okami (Dogs and Wolves of Japan)*; Dr. Noburo Sagara of Waseda University; Dr. Tei Uchida; Mr. Hiroyoshe Saito and Mr. Naoto Kajiwara, author of *My Thoughts on the Akita Dog*.

It was long believed that people first migrated to the Japanese Islands around 4,000 years ago, bringing with them the Jamon culture of hunters. However, more recent archaeological finds indicate that Japanese history dates further back into the Stone Age. A study of reconstructed skeletal remains and fossils from the Jamon Period indicate that domesticated dogs first appeared during this time, and were used for hunting and protection.

Though it is not known whether these dogs had stand-up ears and curled tails, or if they were originally from Japan, it may be assumed that they were related to the present Akita.

The Bronze Age of Yayoi followed the Stone Age. Drawings and artifacts of this period picture dogs with stand-up ears and half-curled tails, and other distinct features of the Japanese type dog.

2

During the reign of Emperor Jinmu (600 B.C.) new dogs were brought from China and Korea.

From this point in history forward, there are many and conflicting theories. However, it is generally accepted that the traditional Japanese type dogs evolved into their various distinctive forms, greatly influenced by their habitat and geographical location. In areas where there were rapidly changing civilizations and exposure to outside influences, the purity of the breed tended to disappear because of much cross-breeding. In general, the Japanese dogs that were declared to be natural monuments came from the remote mountain areas where civilization was slow to make inroads, and where the purity of the dog breeds was maintained.

There are seven breeds of Japanese dogs that were declared as natural monuments, and named according to their place of origin. They were also classified by sizes into large, medium and small dogs. The large dog is the Akita, from the Odate area. There is no other known large Japanese dog surviving today.

The name Akita-Inu (Akita Dog) was not used until September 1931, at which time the Akita was designated as a natural monument. Prior to that time, dogs from the Odate Region were called Odate Dogs. During the Feudal Period these dogs were called Nambu-Inu (Southern Regional Dog).

Those dogs that were used for fighting purposes were called Kuriya-Inu while those used for hunting by the mountain villagers were called Matagi-Inu. The word Matagi refers to hunter. Thus, since ancient times, Japanese dogs were named according to their locale, or their roles as domesticated animals. It seems clear that the direct forebears of the Akita as we know it today were native to Akita Prefecture, the northernmost province on the main Japanese island of Honshu. The historical epicenter of the present-day Akita is the City of Odate in Akita Prefecture.

Several organizations have evolved in Japan that have contributed significantly to the preservation and restoration of the Akita.

During the Dog Fighting Era of the Meiji Period (1868–1912), there was a dog fighting club called Enyukai. The Akita Kyokai was another dog fighting club formed during the Taisho Period (1912–1925).

Akitainu Hozonkai (AKIHO), the largest and most dominant

SHINTORA-GO. Beloved dog of Mr. Yugoro Izumi, circa 1951, the 25th year of the SHOWA. These previously unpublished photos (pages 4–5) are from a collection given to Mr. Lusk by Dr. Keichi Ogasawara of Odate City, Akita Prefecture, Japan.

金號

秋田犬

KIN-GO. Akita dog. Natural Monument Designate.

4

Female Akita. Odate area, circa 1928.

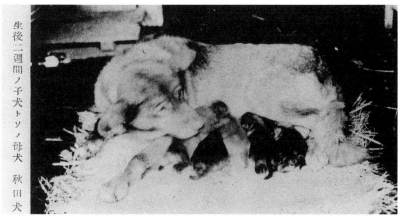

生後二週間ノ子犬トソノ母犬　秋田犬

Akita puppies at two weeks of age. Akita Prefecture, circa 1930.

5

The Stand-off.

Akita club in Japan today, was established in 1927. A branch of the organization was founded in Los Angeles during 1969. Nipponken Hozonkai (NIPPO), was established in 1928, and Akitainu Kyokai (AKIKYO) was established in 1948. Each of the three aforementioned organizations has developed an Akita Breed Standard, and its own Akita Registry.

TAISHO PERIOD, 1912–1925. Dogs being presented to the Emperor Taisho, the father of Emperor Hirohito, as part of his coronation. Odate, 1910.

6

One of the most significant events in the restoration and preservation of the Akita was the tremendous attention commanded throughout Japan and the entire world by the moving story of an Akita dog named Hachi-Ko. No dog before or since has so touched the hearts of people everywhere.

THE AKITA IS BROUGHT TO AMERICA

No story of the Akita would be complete without mention of the rather extraordinary circumstances surrounding the first Akita known to come to America. Years before the Akita caught the eye and fancy of American military occupation personnel in Japan following World War II, a famous American woman discovered and learned to love the unique character and qualities of this magnificent breed. What must have enraptured her most were the spiritual rather than the physical characteristics of the Akita, for she had been blind since birth.

Helen Keller, world-famed scholar, lecturer, author, educator, humanitarian, first visited the Orient and Japan in 1937, where she

Akita City, 1988. *L to R:* Mr. Sugawara, Don Lusk, Dr. Ishigura, Twyla Lusk.

7

commenced a grueling ten-week speaking tour, visiting thirty-nine cities and giving ninety-nine lectures to more than a million people. Her tour would take her eventually to Akita City, a town of about 60,000 residents at that time. During an interview with reporters earlier, she had indicated that she would like to have an Akita dog. The notion probably came to her while in Tokyo where she had learned of the Akita dog Hachi-Ko, and was touched by his story. At Akita City, Mr. Ichire Ogasawara, a member of the Akita Police Department, presented Miss Keller with one of his own new puppies, Kamikaze-Go. It should be remembered that at that time purebred Akitas were virtually nonexistent outside of Akita Prefecture, and very scarce even there.

Kamikaze-Go returned to the United States with Helen Keller aboard the liner *Chichibu Maru*. "Kami," as he was affectionately called, went to live with Helen Keller at her estate in New York. Unfortunately, Kami became ill and died in November of the same year at the tender age of eight months. In June 1939, a second Akita, Kenzan-Go, was sent to Miss Keller from her admirers in Japan. Kenzan-Go lived with Miss Keller until his death in around 1944 or 1945.

So started the strange introduction of the Akita to America, and the ensuing interest in this exotic breed from Japan, which finally culminated in recognition of the Akita in America by the American Kennel Club in 1973.

Three events that in combination contributed significantly to focusing attention on the Akita dog during the two decades preceding World War II were: the saga of Hachi-Ko, the tour of Japan by Helen Keller and her involvement with the breed and the declaration of the Akita as a natural monument. Had these events not occurred, one must wonder if the Akita, as a distinctive and identifiable breed, would have survived.

After the Akita was declared a natural monument, there is ample recorded evidence of a strong surge of activity, in the Odate area in particular, to restore the Japanese Akita to its original state. It is fortunate indeed that the road back for the Akita started in the 1920s; otherwise, World War II, which further decimated the ranks of the breed, would probably have been the final extinction of the Akita dog. That the Akita did survive the Second World War is in

8

itself a miracle, for that great conflict took its toll of dogs as well as people. The ravages of war caused the normal shortages of commodities, and the food shortage rapidly became serious.

The Akita, which consumed the most food among Japanese dogs, suffered greatly, and gradually dwindled in numbers. Dog and cat pelts began to be used to provide cold weather clothing for the military. The large Akita dog thus became a primary target to be captured for such uses. According to dog owners who lived in Akita Prefecture at that time, the Police Department issued orders for dog catchers to go into all of the towns and villages to capture and kill all dogs, except for the Shepherd, which was being used as a military dog. It is said that a considerable number of Akita dogs were captured and clubbed to death. During these dark days of 1941–1945, the Akita was threatened with virtual extinction.

No one knows for sure how many Akitas survived the World War II. One record of postwar dogs is found in the *Akitainu Tokuhon (Akita Dog Textbook)* by Mr. Kiyono. It lists several dogs of the Ichinoseki line, including Ichinoseki-Go, Shintora-Go, Hachiman-Go, Tatenohana-Go, Arawashi-Go and Dainimatsumine-Go. The Dewa line consisted of Raiden-Go, Dewawaka-Go, Taishu-Go, Tatemitsu-Go and Shinmutsu-Go.

According to the Akiho magazine, some of the dogs shown at the 12th Akiho Show in April 1948 were from the wartime period. They include Bushi-Go, Tamazakura-Go, Habubotan-Go, Furuhime-Go, Tomoe-Go and Mitzukaze-Go, all of which were considered as Tokuyu (superior) dogs. There were about sixty Akita entries at this show.

During the period of 1948–1950, many historically famous Akita dogs were produced, including Goromaro-Go (regarded as the most important foundation stud dog in the restoration process), Jiromaru-Go (littermate to Goromaro-Go), Torafusa-Go, Long-Go, Dainikisaragi-Go, Shinsan-Go, Shinko-Go, Tohuko-Go, Arawai-Go, Tsukasa-Go, Kurogani-Go, Kincho-Go, Shinben-Go and Tanihibiki-Go.

As the Akita dog became more popular and increased in numbers, the lineage of the dogs became a matter of great emphasis among the serious breeders. During this period emerged the two main lines (the Ichinoseki and the Dewa), which became the starting

Photo taken in Japan inside the AKIHO show ring.   *Courtesy D. Lusk.*

point for the Akita breed as it gained a first foothold in America during the 1950s and 1960s.

In 1978, I made my first trip to Japan to examine the state of the Akita breed in its country of origin. During that and four subsequent trips, I had the opportunity to see the results of thirty years of a concentrated effort by breeders in Japan to create an Akita of consistent type, conformation and color.

I found the results to be astonishing as to consistency and uniformity. During December 1978, at the annual AKIHO Akita Show I attended in Tokyo, 330 Akitas were presented. There was no question as to breed type or gender, even to the casual observer.

How were the Japanese able to develop such consistency in twenty-five to thirty years? In America we have been breeding Akitas for about forty-five years and, from what I see, lack the elements of consistency. I can only advance an opinion of what has happened differently in Japan and America. In America there does not seem to be a "shared vision" of what the Akita should be in this country.

In Japan there was not only a clear consensus of what they were working toward, but a strong Akita Breed Registry Organization (AKIHO) committed to moving the breed toward a common visualization.

Finally, I think the growing preoccupation with exhibiting and winning in the show ring crystalized by AKC recognition in 1973 has reduced the average Akita fancier's ability to see the Akita in any historical context, past or present, and more importantly has reduced the level of interest in that subject. I suspect that the majority of those breeding Akitas today have little concern with or commitment to sound genetic principles.

I would like to leave you with a single focus. The history of the Akita in America for the next twenty-five years will be written by you and the breeders that follow. Your breed will indeed be a self-fulfilling prophecy.

JAPANESE GRAND CHAMPION AZUMAZAKURA-GO. Born 2/23/60. One of the all-time greats. Sire: J. Gr. Ch. Hachiman-Go; Dam: J. Gr. Ch. Tamakiyo-Go.

2

Great Dogs of Japan
and Their Influence
on the Breed

EXTENSIVE RESEARCH has been done on the
Akita family tree. However, prior to 1930, few records and pictures
are available. In tracing early pedigrees, two names that frequently
appear are **Tochini-Go** and **Babagoma-Go**. These animals are
thought to have given the most early influence to the present main
Akita line in Japan.

Tochini-Go, a male popularly called "Aka," was owned by
Mr. Isumi, the first chairman of AKIHO. Aka was sired by a white
Akita fighting dog called Mitane-Go. His dam, Norogomame-Go,
was red goma in color. (When two words describe a coat color, the
first word is the primary color and the second refers to the color of
the undercoat.) "Red goma" is a red outercoat with a gray undercoat. An early photo reveals one flopped ear and a coiled tail.
Despite the ear fault, he impresses one as being a pure Japanese
dog.

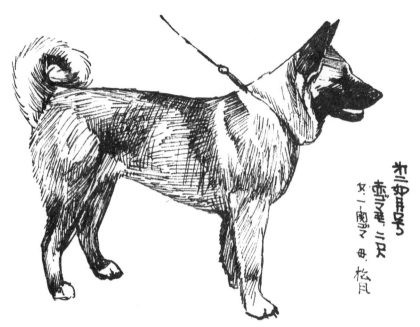

JOGETSU-GO (the second Jogetsu). Sire: Ichinoseki Goma-Go; Dam: Matsukaza-Go. This pen and ink sketch was done in Japan, circa 1950.

The train station at Ichinoseki. Home of the Ichinoseki family and their famous line of Akitas. *Courtesy D. Lusk.*

ICHINOSEKI-AKA-GO (the sire of Goromaru-Go's dam), circa 1893. Sire: Ichinoseki Tora-Go; Dam: Numatate Tora-Go.

Babagoma-Go was a red female owned by Mr. Kunio Ichinoseki of Odate, founder of the famous line that bears his name. Many famous old-time Akitas stem from the Ichinoseki line, which still flows through the blood of today's Akitas.

Ichinoseki Goma-Go, known as **Tsubaki Goma**, was an aka goma–colored male standing 27.5 inches at the withers. He was an imposing animal despite his slight looseness of body. When bred to Futatsui Goma-Go (Matagi line), they produced the famous Goromaru-Go, regarded by many as the most important dog in the effort to bring the breed up to standard after the ravages of World War II.

15

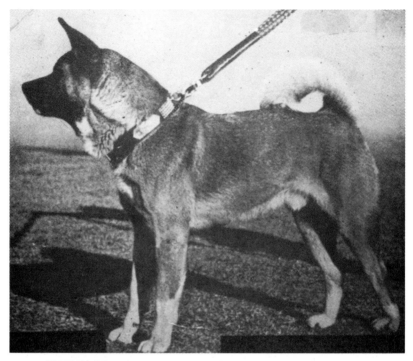

SENZAN-GO, circa 1950. Sire: Shintora-Go; Dam: Dainijogetsu-Go.

Japanese Grand Ch. **Goromaru-Go** was regarded as the ''Ancestor dog that rejuvenated the Akita.'' He and his three littermates were born February 8, 1948. Mr. Susumu Funakoshi bought Goromaru and recalls he was a precocious red-and-white pinto puppy with a large head, longer than average coat and rather small, deepset, triangular-shaped eyes. Goromaru and his brother, the 25-inch **Jiromaru-Go**, were popular in the show ring.

The excellent quality of Goromaru offspring down through the years brought fame to this dog. When bred to the Ohira line of Akitas, e.g., Chimpei-Go and Shiromaru-Go, the results were spectacular, despite warnings from breeders who claimed the country-bred pinto would reproduce his color, which was not in favor at that time, and would throw long coats known as ''Moku.'' However, when Goromaru died at the age of nine in 1956, his fame was such that his funeral was attended by Akita fanciers from all areas of Japan.

五 郎 丸 号

GOROMARU-GO, whelped February 8, 1948. Owner, Mr. Susumu Funakoshi.

		Saburo-Go	Tora-Go
	Jugoro-Go		Oshinai-Go
		Yama-Go	Tora-Go
Ichinoseki Goma-Go			Kuma-Go
		Goma-Go	Tora-Go
	Toshi-Go		Oshinai-Go
		Yama-Go	Tora-Go
			Kuma-Go
		Ichinoseki Toro-Go	Kin-Go
	Ichinoseki Aka-Go		Tama-Go
		Numatate Tora-Go	(unknown)
Futatsui Goma-Go			(unknown)
		Osawaka-Go	(unknown)
	Shirayuki-Go		(unknown)
		Aniaka-Go	(unknown)
			(unknown)

17

Mrs. Funakoshi and the revered pelt of Goromaru-Go. Japan, 1970.

18

DAIUNME-GO was a brindle bitch with a wonderful appearance. According to Shinichi Ishiguro, however, she lost the tip of her left ear when a dog from the adjoining property leaped a fence and attacked her. Therefore, she was not shown.

She was bred, however, and what she produced in her breeding career when bred to Tanigumo-o, Yama-Go and Azumazakura-Go was spectacular: three Meiyosho winners; ten or more Tokuyu winners.

She was beyond a doubt one of the most famous bitches produced in Japan, with her get strengthening the mainstream of Akita dogs in Japan today.

Joan Linderman was privileged to meet Daiunme in 1970. She died when she was 14, on July 14, 1973 (the 48th year of the Showa), at the Iwamatsu Kennel.

			Tanihibiki-Go
		TAMAGUMO-GO	
			Jyurome-Go
DAIUN-GO			
			GOROMARU-GO
		MAKOME-GO	
			ASHUME-GO
			Tanihibiki-Go
		TAMAGUMO-GO	
			Jyurome-Go
KIYOME-GO			
			GOROMARU-GO
		KIYOHIME-GO	
			CHINPEI-GO

19

JAPANESE CH. KUMOMARU. Sire: Nanun-Go; Dam: Makome-Go.

Goromaru was bred to Chimpei-Go in 1950 and produced Kirohime-Go, a lovely red bitch with white mask from Southern Akita Prefecture. She in turn was bred to the brindle dog Tamagumo-Go and produced the bitch Kiyome-Go who, when bred to Daiun, whelped the incomparable bitch **Daiunme-Go**. Daiunme had a luxurious black brindle coat and excellent frame. She was not shown as the result of a freak accident when a neighboring dog leaped a fence and took a bite out of the tip of one ear. However, that did not prevent her, through her offspring, from becoming one of the most admired bitches in recent Japanese Akita records.

Daiunme produced three Meiyosho winners (those dogs who

ICHINOSEKI TORA-GO, whelped Sept. 29, 1932
(red brindle/left ear down)

Kin-Go (pale red)	Tochini-Go (black brindle/ left ear down)	Mitane-Go	unknown unknown
		Norogomame-Go	unknown unknown
	Shiro-Go	Nidaioshinaiyama	Tateisami-Go Goma-Go
		Aka-Go	Hamakaze-Go Aka-Go
Tama-Go (red)	Tochini-Go	Mitane-Go	unknown unknown
		Norogomame-Go	unknown unknown
	Babagoma-Go (red tip)	Goma-Go	Goma-Go Aka-Go
		Aka-Go	Hamakaze-Go Aka-Go

ICHINOSEKI GOMA-GO, whelped April 10, 1943

Jugoro-Go	Saburo-Go	Ichinoseki Tora-Go	Kin-Go Tama-Go
		Oshinai-Go	Tochisan-Go Babagoma-Go
	Yama-Go	Ichinoseki Tora-Go	Kin-Go Tama-Go
		Kuma-Go	Tora-Go Aka-Go
Toshi-Go	Goma-Go	Ichinoseki Tora-Go	Kin-Go Tama-Go
		Oshinai-Go	Tochisan-Go Babagoma-Go
	Yama-go	Ichinoseki Tora-Go	Kin-Go Tama-Go
		Kuma-Go	Tora-Go Aka-Go

KIYOME-GO. Sire: Tamagumo-Go; Dam: Kiyihime-Go. Dam of the famous Daiunme-Go . . . the melding of north and south!

receive the highest award in Japan) in Bankomaru-Go, Kumohibiki-Go and Tamagumome-Go. She also produced ten known Tokuyu winners. These winners were produced in three litters with three different dogs. Daiunme passed away July 14, 1973 (forty-eighth year of the Showa) at the Iwamatsu-so kennel, at fourteen years of age. Joan Linderman had the good fortune to see and spend some moments with Daiunme-Go in 1970 when she was eleven years old. Even then one could see that she had been an outstanding bitch with a charming personality.

Bankomaru's littermate, Nanun-Go, produced the dog Kumo-maru-Go, who in turn produced the beautiful red bitch, Meiyosho winner Tamayu-Go.

Another important Akita was **Tamagumo-Go**, an imposing brindle male sired by Arawashi-Go (Ichinoseki line) and whelped by Sansho-Go (Dewa line). Although he had a number of small faults, his markings, coat and masculinity could not be surpassed. The breadth and depth of his chest was to be admired. This worthy male can be found behind many of today's excellent Japanese Akitas.

The **Dewa line** existed at the same time as the **Ichinoseki line**. It derived its name from the black-tip male Dewa-Go, who was

TAIHO-GO. Mr. Hashimoto described him as an unbelievably beautiful dog. Taiho was owned by Mr. Tatanabe, director of NICHIKO.

TAMAYU-GO. Sire: Kumamaru-Go; Dam: Amabuki-Go. The red Meiyosho winning bitch is pictured in Japan in 1970. Owner, Mr. K. Ichikawa.

born February 1, 1941. It is said the ancestral dog behind him was Tachi-Go, a.k.a. Yari.

According to the late Mr. Naoei Sato, as quoted in *The Akita-inu*, "the Akita dogs of the Dewa line were noted for their large stately build and gentle temperament as household dogs, and yet were firm in their stand when necessary. However, the Dewa line soon began to lose value as a top-quality representative of the Akita dog breed with the appearance of looseness of skin under the throat, loose, baggy lips and other features that led to a departure from the Japanese dog image."

Immediately following World War II, Dewa-Go's great-grand-

KIN-GO, circa 1928. Kin was the first Akita registered with AKIHO. The original of this picture can be seen in Odate at the AKIHO Museum.

DEWA-GO, whelped February 1, 1941. Owned by Mr. Yozaburo Ito.

			Goma-Go
		Aikoku-Go	Aka-Go
	Akagoro-Go		Katsura-Go
		Shiro-Go	Tama-Go
Akidate-Go			(unknown)
		Taro-Go	(unknown)
	OtsutaGoma-Go		(unknown)
		Kuma-Go	(unknown)
			(unknown)
		Katsuhira-Go	(unknown)
	Mutsu-Go		(unknown)
		Goma-Go	(unknown)
Tama-Go			Ichinoseki Tora-Go
		Taka-Go	(unknown)
	Takatorame-Go		(unknown)
		Gin-Go	(unknown)

26

ORYU-GO, whelped in 1953.

			Saburo-Go
		Jugoro-Go	Yama-Go
	Ichinoseki Goma-Go		Goma-Go
		Toshi-Go	Yama-Go
Goromaru-Go			Ichinoseki Tora-Go
		Ichinoseki-Go	Numatate Tora-Go
	Futatsui Goma-Go		Osawaaka-Go
		Shirayuki-Go	Aniaka-Go
			Kurowashi-Go
		Shiranami-Go	Hachi-Go
	Dainishirana-Go		Suihoku-Go
		Akashime-Go	Yamime-Go
Akashihime-Go		Suihoku-Go	Heiku-Go
	Akahime-Go		Yamime-Go
		Yamime-Go	Muchi-Go
			Heitsume-Go

27

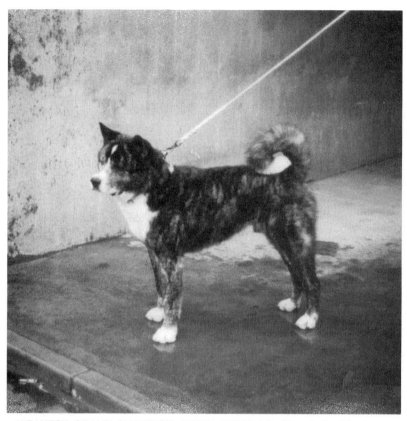

JAPANESE GRAND CHAMPION AZUMA KUMO-GO. Sire: J. Gr. Ch. Azuma Zakura-Go; Dam: J. Gr. Ch. Gyokurei. This famous Meiyosho-winning male was 10 years old at the time. Owned by Taro and Yuriko Matsudo of the famous Tokyo Matsuda Kennels, this dog was also known as Tōun. AKIHO #55270.

Photo by author in Japan.

son Kongo-Go began a show and breeding career that was said to have dominated the dog scene. The Dewa line descended from Dewa-Go to Dewawaka-Go, Taishu-Go, Kongo-Go and Kincho-Go, in that order.

The kurogoma color, black sesame, dominated the Dewa line and was genetically very powerful. It held for generations. According to one source, Kongo's owner, the late Mr. Hikashi Hashimoto, went so far as to label Kongo's picture with the words "Kongo-Go, the National Treasure."

Japanese Grand Ch. Kongo-Go was born in 1947 at the Heirakudo Kennel of Mr. Ryonosuke Hiraizumi at Odate City, Japan.

28

JAPANESE GRAND CHAMPION TENSEI. Sire: Tōun; Dam: Fumihime. Tensei was the sire of Haruhime.

JAPANESE GRAND CHAMPION TANIHIBIKI-GO. Born 10/25/50. Sire: Goromaru-Go; Dam: Shiromaru-Go. Another great Japanese Akita.

TAMAGUMO-GO, a.k.a. TAMAKUMO-GO. This outstanding brindle, born 12/13/50, was the fourth Akita to earn a Meiyosho from AKIHO. Owned by Mr. Riyosuke Tadamoto, he was a major contributor to the breed.

So popular, in fact, were Kongo and his offspring, that they dominated the show scene in the post–World War II period.

Although his name appears often in many of the early pedigrees of early imports into the United States, here, as in Japan, the number of dogs of this type has declined. Kongo-Go died at the Hashimoto home in September 1955.

Although high awards were given Kongo and Kincho during the time breeders were trying to restore the Akita dog to what it had been in the past, the Dewa line declined by degrees.

It is said that starting in 1955, the Unjiyo-Go line dominated the scene, winning for a period. Such outstanding dogs were Unjiyo-Go, Muchi-Go, Hachiman-Go, Azumazakura-Go, Azumagumo-Go and Bankomaru-Go.

Unjiyo-Go was used widely as a stud dog and it is said that his offspring dominated the young dog classes at shows. In maturity they fell short of the mark. **Muchi-Go**, born in 1956, was awarded the AKIHO's revered Sakuohutsukorosho award for producing outstanding dogs, as were Goromaru-Go and Kiyohime-Go. It was the pinto Muchi who popularized the red-and-white dogs. He in turn

金　剛　號　（牡）—平楽洞

六 歳 当 時

KONGO-GO. Born in 1947.

			Akitate-Go
		Dewa-Go	Tama-Go
	Dewawaka-Go		(unknown)
		Kuzugoma-Go	(unknown)
Taishu-Go			Goma-Go
		Tokiwa-Go	Nagata-Go
	Takahime-Go		Noritsu-Go
		Maru-Go	Hayaguchigoma-Go
			Akitate-Go
		Dewa-Go	Tama-Go
	Dewawaka-Go		(unknown)
		Kuzugoma-Go	(unknown)
Tatemitsu-Go			Tatetaro-Go
		Tategoro-Go	(unknown)
	Kikumaru-Go		Habutaro-Go
		Tatetorama-Go	Tate-Go

32

MUCHI-GO. Born 3/30/56. Sire: Unjo-Go; Dam: Kiyohime-Go. Breeder, Dr. Kinichi Ogasawara. Owner, Mr. Yoshiki Yagi.

sired Hachiman-Go, an outstanding red male whose features were a good deal more classical.

FAITHFUL HACHIKO

One of the most significant events in the restoration and preservation of the Akita was the tremendous attention commanded throughout Japan and the entire world by the moving story of an Akita dog named Hachiko. No dog before or since has so touched the hearts of people everywhere.

Meiyosho winner KUMOHIBIKI-GO. Sire: Tanikumo-Go; Dam: Daiunme-Go. Pictured as a youngster.

Hachiko was born in Akita in November 1923. He was brought to Tokyo in January 1924 and was kept by Mr. Eisaburo Uyeno, who then held the Chair of Professorship in the Department of Agriculture at the Imperial University.

Mr. Uyeno was very kind to Hachi and the dog reciprocated in such a way that they became great (sic) friends. When Hachi grew up he became a fine specimen of a large-size Japanese breed. He

HACHIKO. As preserved and displayed at the Japanese Museum of Natural Science, Tokyo, Japan. *Photo by D. Lusk.*

"THE FAITHFUL HACHIKO."

35

特優犬　　十四女号　（牝）　　雲丸×白鵬女

JAPANESE GRAND CHAMPION TOSHIME-GO. Circa 1970. Well-known brindle Meiyosho winner, owned by Mrs. Shinkai. Pictured "for show."

HAKUHO-GO. Sire: Azuma-Go; Dam: Takehime-Go. Born 10/5/54. Bred by Mr. Arisawa. Owned by Chiosi Kusaka.

had a fine cream-colored coat with pointed ears and a curly tail, standing two feet tall (sic) and weighing 92 pounds.

It was Hachi's custom to accompany his master every morning wet or fine to the Shibuya Station and wait for his return in the afternoon when the master and the dog would (sic) happily come home together.

This friendship lasted until one day in May 1925. On that day Hachi saw his master disappear among the crowd in the usual way at Shibuya Station, but that was the last he saw of him, for the master was taken ill while at work and died before he was brought home. The sad event occurred when Hachi was just over 16 months old, but Hachi never forgot his master. Hachi went daily after that to Shibuya Station, apparently in the hope of finding Mr. Uyeno.

Sometimes he would stay there for several days without returning home at all. The patient search lasted until March 8, 1934, when Hachi died on the very spot where he saw his master last. However,

UJO-GO. Sire: Fujitaro-Go; Dam: Shirame-Go. One of the earliest well-known reds.

even before Hachi's death, people who saw the pathetic figure of this faithful creature growing old day by day were so deeply moved by the sight that they decided to erect a statue in memory of this noble animal.

In April 1934 a beautiful bronze statue executed by the famous sculptor, Mr. Ando Teru, was erected in front of the Shibuya Station, but in 1945 this statue was regretably taken down by order of the Army and was later melted down for use in making war weapons.

Soon after the end of the war a plan for re-erecting the the statue was contemplated and it was then decided to entrust the making of the new statue to Mr. Ando Takeshi, son of Mr. Ando Teru, who unfortunately was killed in one of the air raids during the war.

The new statue is similar in size and shape to the old one and it will no doubt be instrumental in perpetuating the sweet memory of faithful Hachiko.

The story as printed is the actual inscription on the base of the statue itself, as seen and copied by the Lusks while in Tokyo in 1976.

KUMOHIBIKI-GO. As an older dog in Japan, 1970.

Brownie at six and a half years of age won Best in Show, handled by Carol Foti.

3

The Akita in America

EARLY CONTRIBUTIONS AND THE ROAD TO AMERICAN KENNEL CLUB RECOGNITION

Why is the Akita in the United States? How did the breed reach our shores? Ironically, it took a war between two countries to bring the Akita to our land. Servicemen stationed in Occupied Japan were captivated by the breed's beauty; some simply wanted to bring home a "live" souvenir. A few who acquired Akitas entered them in the Japan Kennel Club all-breed shows. Though showing was a hobby, some champions were made who were used in breeding programs on return to the United States.

Most of the first Akitas settled on our east and west coasts, destination points of ships returning home. California saw the largest influx of Akitas step foot on American soil. The state still boasts the greatest numbers of the breed. As our servicemen began to pick up the threads of their former lives, the animals they brought back quite naturally took a backseat in future plans. Even so, enough interest was aroused to create a market for more Akitas. The breed grew slowly, and much like some breed purchasers today, in many instances, servicemen's families were unprepared for this new addition. These people ultimately sold or gave away their Akitas to people with more adequate facilities. Some of the Akitas were bred once, many were bred several times and some not at all.

It is unfortunate the Akita was brought here before Japanese fanciers began to make strides in improving the breed. Had Akitas come into the United States in the 1970s, the time when military personnel Mr. and Mrs. D. D. Confer and Karen Keene brought in the famous Grand Champions Haruhime and Teddy Bear of Toyohashi Seiko, we would possibly have had a more uniform type of dog here today.

EARLY BREED CLUBS AND THEIR IMPACT ON THE BREED

Our first breed clubs surfaced, disappeared and resurfaced. They changed their names, memberships, Standards and club formats. Members were not "professional" dog breeders. For many, the Akita was their first dog. Because material from Japan was not readily available, breeding programs were a matter of guesswork. Culling was virtually unheard of, and even so, few persons knew what to cull or how.

In 1952, the Akita Dog Association of America was established in Southern California and had a closed membership. Mr. M. Kelly Spellmeyer was founder and secretary.

On June 5, 1956, eleven Akita fanciers, who among them owned thirty Akitas, held the first general meeting of the second club organized, the Akita Kennel Club. Three years later, on September 6, 1959, it was suggested "Kennel" be omitted from the name. In November 1959, steps were taken to achieve nonprofit corporation status under the new name, the Akita Club of America. Using forms patterned after those of the American Kennel Club, a registration file was set up for foreign and American-bred Akitas. Clyde Brown was president. Finally, on August 23, 1960, state of California papers were endorsed and filed, and the Parent Club was born.

A month earlier, a splinter group from the club had started yet another new club, Akita Breeders Association, with fourteen charter members. On the heels of its formation, a letter from attorney J. F. Cuneo informed them they were infringing on the rights of Mr. and Mrs. Lee Fisher, who, on January 17, 1956, had the name Akita Breeders Association registered in Los Angeles County. However, we have no documented knowledge that a working club was actually formed. The splinter group threw up its hands in exasperation and contacted Mr. Spellmeyer of Akita Dog Association of America. He agreed to open that group's membership to them. The pot began to boil over.

The new Parent Club accused Mr. Spellmeyer's new members of taking the Stud Book and missing registrations. According to our records, this was apparently resolved. In 1961, a newsletter, published by the Akita Club of America, Inc., contained within its pages a motion made once again to accept the splinter group back into the fold of ACA, whose membership swelled to approximately sixty-two.

As time passed, attempts were made to cement old relationships. However, in March 1963, Charles W. Rubinstein led another group away from the Parent Club. Although Mr. Rubinstein left the scene and went on to other interests, the newly organized club named itself American Akita Breeders. Its membership boasted such well-known names in Akitadom as Samuel and Barbara Mullen, William Conway, Anita Powell and Camille Kam.

The newly established AAB added dimension and strength to the breed. Their shows were well organized and all had good attendance. Members remained unified until a short time before the Akita breed was recognized by the American Kennel Club.

THE MISCELLANEOUS CLASS AT AKC SHOWS

On July 13, 1955, the Akita was granted approval by the American Kennel Club to be shown in the Miscellaneous Class at licensed all-breed shows. The records indicate the first Akitas were shown in this class on January 29, 1956, at the Orange Empire Kennel Club show in San Bernardino, California. Mrs. Meyers judged. The records also indicate that thirteen Akitas took part in twenty-one licensed shows and placed 50 times out of 168 possible placings their first year in Miscellaneous competition.

The first Akita ever shown in Miscellaneous Class at a prestigious Westminster Kennel Club show was Teruhime-Go, a red bitch who was brought into this country when she was eighteen months old. She placed first. The press had a field day with "the unique breed from Japan," and owners Mr. and Mrs. Thomas Hamilton couldn't have been more proud.

Miscellaneous competition served as an apprenticeship for the Akita. Club point systems were set up for the Akitas who were shown. The judges were exposed to the breed and owners learned ring procedure. Everyone found out what it was like to have patience. After seventeen years in the Miscellaneous ring, the breed was finally recognized!

THE ROAD TO RECOGNITION

That the road to recognition was filled with potholes is quite obvious. When the bickering between the clubs reached a boiling point, new members with a fresh outlook said, "Enough is enough. Let's straighten out this mess!" An upheaval in the ranks ensued when questions pertaining to the validity of the registration bureau arose. Members demanded the right to have the Stud Book opened at general meetings, a reasonable request.

It had long been felt that one of the major stumbling blocks to recognition was the less than peaceful existence between the American Akita Breeders and the Akita Club of America. Although attempts had been made to pull the two organizations together, it finally took a nine-person arbitration committee on October 4, 1969, to effect a merger. Representing the Japanese community, Walter Imai served as mediator. The goal was to create one united Akita club. The attempt was thwarted by factions within the ACA.

A short time later, some members of the Akita Club of America formed The Insight Group. Frederick W. Pitts, M.D., famous neurosurgeon, had an Akita and was persuaded to join the cause. The Group decided to present a slate of officers for the coming ACA election that would bring about the needed merger and provide strict interpretation of club constitution and bylaws. Though election proceedings were unpleasant, the slate won. Club relations im-

THE AMERICAN KENNEL CLUB
51 MADISON AVENUE
NEW YORK, N.Y. 10010

October 24, 1972

NOTICE

REGISTRATION OF THE AKITA

By action of the Board of Directors of The American Kennel Club, the Akita has been admitted to registry in the AKC Stud Book, effective immediately.

Registration of Akitas now in the United States will generally be limited to dogs that have already been individually registered or litter registered with the Akita Club of America.

Special AKC registration application forms for the registration of foundation stock for the breed are available on request by writing to:

Mrs. Kay Greisen, Registrar   Mrs. Barbara Uyeda
Akita Club of America   Akita Club of America
P. O. Box 3742, University Station   1936 Armacost Avenue
Charlottesville, VA 22902   West Los Angeles, CA 90025

All such applications, when completed, must be mailed to Mrs. Greisen at the above address. Mrs. Greisen will forward them to The American Kennel Club.

For a dog from an ACA registered litter that has not been individually registered, the completed ACA registration form must be attached to the special application.

No fee will be required with a special application to register a dog that has been individually registered by the ACA -- the fee will be paid by ACA for such dogs. Check or money order for $3.00 must accompany each special application to register a dog from an ACA registered litter that has not yet been individually registered. The fee for registering an imported Akita whelped outside the U.S.A. that has not been registered with ACA will be $10.00.

If you have imported an Akita whelped outside the U.S.A. that has not yet been registered with ACA -- or if you intend to import an Akita -- write to the Registrar, Mrs. Greisen, for instructions, giving her the name of the dog's country of birth. The American Kennel Club plans to register Akitas imported from Japan under policies that conform with present ACA policies -- but only as long as The American Kennel Club Stud Book is open for the registration of foundation stock. Thereafter, the only imports that will be eligible for AKC registration will be those that meet regular American Kennel Club policies applying to imported dogs whelped outside the U.S.A.

45

AMERICAN KENNEL CLUB
51 MADISON AVENUE
NEW YORK, N. Y. 10010

WILLIAM F. STIFEL
EXECUTIVE SECRETARY

October 12, 1973

Mrs. Joan M. Linderman, President
Akita Club of America
18225 Sunburst Drive
Northridge, California 91324

Dear Mrs. Linderman:

Please be advised that by action of our Board of Directors at its recent meeting, the Stud Book will be closed to further registration of Akitas and Bichons Frises as foundation stock on February 28, 1974.

On and after March 1, 1974, Akitas and Bichons Frises will be registrable only under the regular registration procedures of The American Kennel Club.

Notice of this action will be published in the December 1973 and January 1974 issues of Pure-Bred Dogs American Kennel Gazette.

Very truly yours,

William F. Stifel
Executive Secretary

WFS:er
c.c. Mrs. Leajoan Schultz, Secretary
Mrs. Kay Greisen, Registrar

proved, ACA and AAB had a successful merger and a fair editorial policy was established for the newsletter.

On February 13, 1971, the club registrar resigned. President Pitts appointed a committee to take over. With Monica Vogl as chairperson and President Pitts and three other members serving, the Stud Book comprised 3,082 entries after it was updated per American Kennel Club regulations. Kay Greisan eventually replaced Monica Vogl and stayed with the job until recognition. According to President Pitts, "The credibility of our Stud Book is the lifeblood of this club, the purity of the Akita breed in this country and the key to recognition by the American Kennel Club. I believe the proposals I have outlined will re-establish confidence in the registration process."

The year 1971 was an exciting one. John Brownell, then vice-president of the AKC, met with Akita Club of America's board of directors. The workers kept working and a lot of paperwork was completed. But it was not until receipt of the following two letters that we knew recognition was totally ours.

Am/Mex/Can/Int. (CACIB) Ch. GIN-GIN'S HAIYAKU-GO OF SAKUSAKU, ROM, sired by Ch. Sakusaku's Tom Cat-Go, ROM × Shimi Kuma, ROM. Bred to very few select bitches, this handsome brindle made an impact on the breed. His look, type, charisma and genes gave the beed a shot in the arm, as did those of his paternal granddam, the incomparable Haru Hime.

4

Akitas in America— Past and Present

"When I judged in Japan in 1959, I told them I thought they had a great export commodity in the Akita."
—Maxwell Riddle

THE EARLY DAYS

The Akita Club of America Registry is numbered from 100 on. The male dog **Nikko-Go**, born March 13, 1952, is the first entry. Nikko was a combination of Ichinoseki and Dewa lines and was brought into the United States by Lionel Fishman. Although we have no record of his being bred, pictures portray him as being a well-put-together Akita.

The first stud to have an impact on early American breeding programs was **Homare no Maiku-Go**. Homare was born on July 10, 1953, at the Shitara kennel in Japan, and was imported by Lee Fisher. Our records indicate he produced four litters, two out of

49

MAJOR and CINDY, owned by Mr. and Mrs. R. Pattee. These two Akitas are in the background of Ch. Kuro Panzu Maru No Asago ROM.

MAJOR	Wakagimi	Daigo	Gomaiwa Mtsuhikari
		Kiyohime	Kodewa Shinichimaru
	Sachihime	Kodo	Fujiryu Harukaze
		Tamamo	Fuji Kitahime
CINDY	Kamikaze	Taiko Maru	Shingoma Chima
		Hamahime	Shinhama Shinhime
	Kiyome	Okin	Kincho Takahime
		Kiyoryu	Fudo Shintamazakura

50

Mr. and Mrs. Lee Fisher arriving from Japan with HOMARE and TAMAFUJI.

HOMARE	Taro-Go	Araiwa-Go	Dainidewa-Go Iwa-Go
		Fukuju-Go	Shintaro-Go Ichimaru-Go
	Ace Hashimoto	Kongo-Go	Taishu-Go Tatemitsu-Go
		Haname	Kinzan-Go Akitora-Go
TAMAFUJI	Fujigoro-Go	Goromaru-Go	Ichinoseki Goma-Go Futatsuigoma-Go
		Fuji-Go	Oji-Go Kocho-Go
	Kinki-Go	Kincho-Go	Kongo-Go Asahime-Go
		Kinterume-Go	Kincho-Go Teruhime-Go

51

breedings to Tamafugi-Go no Tokyo and one each resulting in breedings to Fukuchiyo-Go and Shunki Kodomo no Akita Ken. Homare's undercoat was fawn, with outer layer and guard hairs being black. His pedigree shows the Dewa line in the background. Homare bred to the import Fukuchiyo-Go, produced the bitch Gin-Joo-Go of Triple K. When bred to Mr. and Mrs. Guarino's import male, Japanese Grand Ch. Kinsho-Go, she whelped three bitches, Akarui Kokoro, Triple K Shina Ningyo and Haiiro Kitsune.

Emma Jung purchased Triple K Shina Ningyo and bred her to Maru Kinsei no Suna-Go. One of their offspring, Triple K Ginsei Shimo, was sold to William Conway, who owned Triple K Shogo. These two produced Mex. Ch. Kinsei Suna Nihon no Taishi, CD. He in turn sired Mex. Am. Ch. Fukumoto's Ashibaya Kuma, ROM.

AKARUI KOKORO. Sire: J. Gr. Ch. Kinsho-Go; Dam: Gin Joo of Triple K. Kokoro was the dam of Akita Tani's Tatsumaki ROM.

KANPUZAN-GO, import. At nine months.

			Tochi-Go
		Shinun-Go	
			Hidekiyo-Go
	Shinzan-Go		
			Kumohibiki-Go
		Kumo-Go	
			Chiakihime-Go
Kanpunzan-Go			
			Kunishinobu-Go
		Nobutome-Go	
			Ginryume-Go
	Tamame-Go		
			Kumokake-Go
		Kotohime-Go	
			Torame-Go

TOMONOBU-GO. Stateside AKIHO Tokoyu winner owned by Kenji and Grace Kusumoto, who were among the original founders of the Los Angeles AKIHO branch and Akita fanciers for many years.

Haiiro Kitsune and Akarui Kokoro were both acquired by Mr. and Mrs. Al Harrell. Kokoro was bred to her sire Kincho-Go and produced Shoyo-Go. Bred back to his dam, he produced the male Akita Tani's Tatsumaki, ROM, who appears in quite a few early pedigrees. Shoyo's influence can be seen in the Kaluzniacki kennel in Arizona, where many show winners have been produced.

When Walter Kam came home from Japan on the aircraft carrier USS *Shangri-La,* he brought Triple K kennel's two foundation Akitas, Goronishiki-Go and the forementioned Fukuchiyo-Go, whose first breeding brought forth a male, Triple K Hayai Taka. When Hayai Taka was bred to Joan and Jerry Linderman's bitch

JIMARS HIKAU OF MARU, dam of Ichiban Mitsubachi CD.

Ichiban Mitsubachi CD, they produced the bitch Mex. Ch. Sakusaku Gorotsuki-Go, ROM, call name "Goro." Goro in turn was bred to Ch. Gin-Gin Haiyaku-Go of Sakusaku and together produced Ch. Sakusaku's Perfect Pearl, ROM, Ch. Sakusaku's Domino-Go, Ch. Sakusaku's Goro, Ch. Sakusaku's Hinode-Go and Ch. Sakusaku's Uncle Lewis, all from one litter.

The Am. Can. Mex. CACIB Ch. Gin-Gin Haiyaku-Go of

Am/Mex Ch. FUKUMOTO'S ASHIBAYA KUMA ROM, handled by Harold Hunt; Mex. Ch. SAKUSAKU GOROTSUKI-GO ROM, handled by Susan Linderman Sanett. Dogs won Best of Breed and Best of Opposite Sex at a Specialty Match.

Sakusaku, ROM (Ch. Sakusaku's Tom Cat-Go, ROM, ex Mex. Ch. Shimi Kuma), known to Akita fanciers as ''Chester,'' was not bred often. However, he had an outstanding show career. He was Best of Breed more than 200 times and had over fifty Group placings. His early show and breeding career was with Sakusaku kennel, and later with Date Tensha kennel on the East Coast. Chester's maternal grandfather, the pinto import Toryu-Go, was of Goromaru lineage. Bred several times to Triple K Yoko, he and his progeny are found in the pedigrees of many present-day Akitas.

Tom Cat's brother, Ch. Tusko's Kabuki, had an outstanding show career. His sisters, Sakusaku's Tiger Lily and Tusko's Star, also did well as producers.

Ed Strader brought Japanese Grand Ch. Teruhide into this country on completion of his tour of duty in Japan. He garnered Teruhide's Japanese title while he and his dog were still in Japan. A well-structured pinto dog, Teruhide was not a tall Akita but was within the Standard for the breed. He eventually went to live with Mr. and Mrs. A. Harrell, who bred him to Kogata Takara (Fuji Akashi ex Kumiko). Parnassus Meiyo of Akita Tani, successful in the Miscellaneous ring, was from that breeding. When Meiyo was bred to Akita Tani's Shoyo-Go, the well-known male Akita Tani's Makoto was whelped from that union. Makoto is behind many of the Akita Tani kennel progeny.

The two males the red Tochifuji and the red-and-white pinto Hozan were brought into the United States by their owners, Rocklaine Imports. After several changes of ownership, Tochifuji was acquired by Mr. and Mrs. Robert Judd. Hozan went to Ivan Wong. Tochifuji brought some Ichinoseki blood to our shores. Hozan had a brief but brilliant show career. Unfortunately, he was killed in an automobile accident. Tochifuji-Go on the West Coast and Shiroi O'Sama-Go on the East Coast were early major contributing factors toward disbursing the Goromaru-Go bloodline in the United States.

Shiroi O'Sama-Go, a.k.a. White King-Go Gobunso, and Aka Goma Joo, a.k.a. Jyo, were the original O'Shea Akitas. Lil O'Shea had raised Pomeranians for thirty years prior to receiving White King for Christmas in 1962. She and her husband, William, later bought Jyo. Three litters were produced by White King and Jyo. One of their most famous offspring was Issei Riki Oji-Go, who, when bred to Kuma's Akai Kosho-Go out of Krug's Santo, produced Mitsu Kuma's Tora Oji-Go, a top winning male when the breed was first shown in licensed rings in 1973. Mitsu Kuma's Tora Oji-Go was the foundation male for Terry Wright's kennel in Maryland. She acquired him from Mr. and Mrs. Samuel Mullen in 1970.

The Mullens started their breeding program with the bitch Kuma Akai Kosho. When bred to the O'Shea's Issei Riki Oji-Go, they produced such Akitas as Mitsu Kuma's Splashdown, Mitsu Kuma's Moonbeam and the three Mitsu Kuma champions Tora, Tiki and Kash.

EAST COAST FOUNDATIONS

A lot of today's East Coast Akitas have the dog Prince Jo, CD, and the bitch Sheba in their pedigrees. Prince Jo was the foundation dog for the Sakura kennel of Mr. and Mrs. Robert Miller. A breeding to Michiko of Kensha, CD, gave them their Ch. Sakura's Bushi, CD. Sheba, owned by Mr. and Mrs. Francis Krug, whelped Krug's Santo as a result of her breeding to Goyokushu of Tojo. When Santo was bred to the imported bitch Karatachi, the result was Krug's Sotto, a well-known male. Both Santo and Sotto were used frequently on the East Coast.

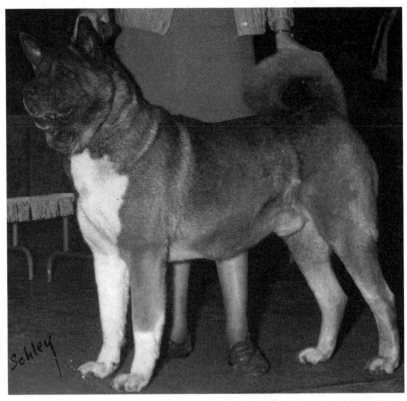

AKITA TANI'S SHOYO-GO, bred and owned by Akita Tani Kennels of Al and Liz Harrell.

		J. Gr. Ch. Kongo-Go
	J. Gr. Ch. Kincho-Go	
		Asahime
J. Gr. Ch. Kinsho-Go		
		Fudo-Go
	Shirayuki	
		Yuki-Go
		J. Gr. Ch. Kincho-Go Abe
	J. Gr. Ch. Kinsho-Go	
		Shirayuki
Akarui Kokoro		
		Homare no Maiku-Go
	Gin Joo of Triple K	
		Fukuchiyo

Japanese Grand Champion TEDDY BEAR OF TOYOHASHI SEIKO. Born 9/13/65 in Japan. Owned by Karen Ann Keen.

		Hachi	Kuma-Go
	Dai of Garyusu		Terumaru-Go
		Hatsume	Jiro-Go
Daio of Toyohashi Seiko			Manryu-Go
		Seibun	Ayahikari-Go
	Aruma of Toyohashi Seiko		Shakauchi-Go
		Yukihime	Tetsumaro-Go
			Fukusumi-Go
		Seibun	Ayahikari-Go
	Taiho of Mikawa Asahi		Shakauchi-Go
		Ayame	Seibun
Shuri of Mikawa Asahi			Yukihime-Go
		Dai of Garyuso	Hachi-Go
	Mutsuhime of Toyohashi Seiko		Hatsume-Go
		Aruma of Toyohashi Seiko	Seibun
			Yukihime-Go

59

Yamakumo, owned by Bill and Barbra Walker, and originally founded in 1970, remains the oldest active Akita kennel in New England. In 1976, the Walkers acquired Yokosa's Kenzan Kahn (Ch. Sakusaku's Tom Cat-Go ex Ch. Matsu Kaze's Gin Kakoro). Kahn brought a dark, luxurious coat to the breeding program as well as a distinctive head and substantial size. A popular stud dog, his most famous offspring was Ch. Tobe's Abracadabra, a Best in Show winner.

White Paw Akitas, founded in 1973 by Bill and Lisa Burland, reflected a bi-coastal approach to breeding with a California foundation bitch, Ch. Golden Sun's Rising Star, bred to East Coast Ch. Mitsu Kuma's Tora Oji-Go. The resulting litter produced Ch. White Paws Jazzman, the first Group-placing Akita in New England.

JAG Akitas, founded in 1973 by Joy Girardi with the foundation bitch Ch. Sakura's Bejin, also followed the bi-coastal approach by breeding Bejin to California's Ch. Sakusaku's Tom Cat-Go. This breeding produced Ch. JAG's Caeser. The program expanded to include a Matsu Kaze female bred to Ch. Tobe's Peking Jumbo, which produced Ch. JAG's Hercules, who subsequently produced Ch. JAG's Lois-T, who is the dam of the Best in Show winner, Ch. Tobe's Return of the Jedi, one of the top winning Akitas in the breed's history.

Ketket's Tiger Bear, CD, and Kanpuzan-Go were two imports who had an impact on the breed in America in the 1970s. Tiger Bear sired Kitamaru, who has contributed greatly to the breed in the Midwest. Kanpuzan-Go was bred to Ch. Triple K Chiyo. Out of this union came Ch. Triple K Shoyu-Go, CD. Shoyu in turn sired Ch. Hashi's Satoshi Awoyama.

THE BEGINNING OF ONE AMERICAN KENNEL
as told by Sandy Batausa

I was raised among dogs in Hawaii all my early years. My first Akita was a gift to me from my parents, Hiroshi (George) and Shizuko (Mildred) Kimoto, when I was sixteen years old. My dad always loved animals and had a fantastic way of training them. As a self-taught handler, he desired a guard dog personality to protect

60

L to R: SHIROI O-SANA-GO and AKAGOMA JYO-GO owned by Bill and Lillian O'Shea. Shiroi was also known as Tomodachi and White-King-Go.

			Goromaru-Go
		Tamihibiki-Go	
	Tochihibiki-Go		Shiromaru-Go
		Kiyomaru-Go	Goromaru-Go
			Kaoru-Go
Shiroi O-Sana-Go			
		Rikimaru-Go	Tanigumo-Go
	Nisikigi-Go		Fujiname-Go
		Tanime-Go	Tanihibiki-Go
			Marunime-Go

L to R: Ch. MITSU KUMA'S TORA OJI-GO pictured at six years of age with his son, Ch. WHITE PAW'S JAZZMAN, at seven months. This pair was the first father-and-son Group placing Akitas. Terri Wright showed Tora; Bill Burland showed his Jazzman.

AM CH. KIN KO, ROM. Bred by T. Shiramizu and owned by B. Hunt.

			Kumo Hibiki
		Tama Hibiki	
			Tora Bo
	Muso Maru		
			Ryo Sei
		Man Ryu	
			Dai-Ni Haku Man
CH. KIN KO, ROM			
			Tochi Hibiki
		Senko Maru	
			Shiun
	Tsubaki Maru Hime		
			Ten Zan
		Bun Jo	
			Bun Ri

63

CH. SAKUSAKU's TOM CAT-GO.

			Dai of Garyuso
		Daio Of Toyohashi Seiko	
	J. Gr. Ch. Teddy Bear of Toyohashi Seiko		Akuma of Toyohashi Seiko
			Taiho Of Mikawa Asahi
		Shuri of Mikawa Asahi	
Ch. Sakusaku's Tom Cat-Go, ROM			Mutsuhime of Toyohashi Seiko
			Tōun
		J. Gr. Ch. Teng Haru	
	J. Gr. Ch. Haru Hime, ROM		Fumi Hime
			Yoshi Tora
		O Tora Hikari Jo	
			Mutsuhime

YUKAN NO OKII YUBI, ROM.

Triple K Shogo

Mex. Ch. Kinsei Suna Nihon No Taishi, CD

Triple K Ginsei Shimo

Am/Mex Ch. Fukumoto's Ashibaya Kuma, ROM

Mex. Ch. Triple K Hayai Taka

Mex. Ch. Triple K Miko

Mex. Ch. Triple K Shina Ningy

Yukan No Okii Yubi, ROM

Rikimaru

Sakusaku's Tanuki-Go, CD

Ichiban Mitsubachi, CD

Toyo-No Namesu Joo, ROM

J. Gr. Ch. Teng Haru a.k.a. Tōun

J. Gr. Ch. Haru Hime, ROM

Otorahikarijo

65

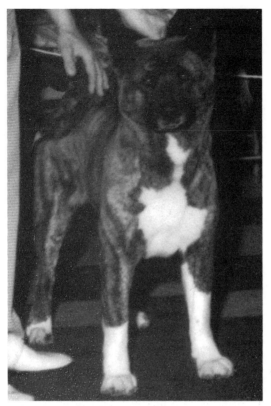

Ch. KETKET'S TIGGER NO NAN CHAO, ROM, owner Hank Janicki.

                                    Ch. Sakusaku's Tom Cat-Go, ROM
                      Ch. Gin-Gin Haiyaku-Go of Sakusaku, ROM
                                    Mex. Ch. Shimi Kuma, ROM
Ch. Sakusaku's Uncle Louie
                                    Mex. Ch. Triple "K" Hayai Taka
                      Mex. Ch. Sakusaku's Gorotsuki-Go, ROM
                                    Ichiban Mitsubachi C.D.
                                    Ch. Sakusaku's Tom Cat-Go, ROM
                      Ch. Gin-Gin Haiyaku-Go of Sakusaku, ROM
                                    Mex. Ch. Shimi Kuma, ROM
Ch. Sakusaku's Diamond Lil
                                    Jap. G. Ch. Teddy Bear of Toyohashi Seiko
                      Sakusaku's Tiger Lily, ROM
                                    J. Gr. Ch. Haru-Hime, ROM

66

Ch. NAN CHAO's SAMURAI NO CHENKO, ROM, owner, Bill Byers.

Erai Kuma of Katshima

Ch. Kazoku's Chenandoh, CD

Kazoku Koka No Hoseki

Akemis Buf-Lo-Go

Shima-Go

Azuma Mune Hiro

Mare Tenshi
Ketket's Tiger Bear, CD

Koka No Hosaki

Ch. Kita Maru

Ch. Remwoods's Koyiko No Nan Chao, CD

Asagao's Chuibukai

Ch. Sakura's Bushi, CD

Ch. Krug's Shumi Go Ditmore

67

his coral jewelry business and store stationed in Hawaii. His business also involved traveling to Japan selling and buying jewelry. Forty-four years ago, my father began his love affair with the Akita and passed this legacy on to me. While he owned several Kongo-type Akitas during the years, he settled upon importing the pair of Akitas Shiro Maru-Go, son of the incomparable Kumo Maru-Go, and a bitch, Mine Hime-Go, granddaughter of Daiunme-Go, the premier bitch of Japan. (Shiro Maru-Go was also the great-grandson of Daiunme-Go.)

A breeding between Shiro Maru-Go and Mine Hime-Go produced our Cha-Iro-No-Kuma in 1969. He was bred to Kisetsu-Go to produce Tane Matsu-Go, ROM. This white bitch was a ROM from only two litters, one sired by Ch. Gaylee's O'Kaminaga, ROM, the other with Ch. Toyo-No Charlie Brown, ROM.

I dedicated my breeding program to my deceased father, who gave me the seeds to plant. Our kennel has done three outcrosses, otherwise we remain true in our program to the Kumo-Maru line. My father saw the great Kumo Maru-Go. He said every muscle rippled when this Akita was presented. His stud fee was high for that day and he was so well trained he could breed at the snap of the fingers. He had eyes "like Satan," almond-shaped to the maximum, the story goes. His owner was offered $10,000 to $15,000 to bring him to the dog show in Chicago and allow American exhibitors to see him, but the owner turned it down because he was fearful of not getting his Akita back.

My father ran his business from home with an open front for shoppers to buy. He needed no security except for his Akita dogs, who kept their eyes on all visitors and were trained by my dad. People would come just to see the Akitas.

Author's note: We are grateful for having Sandy Batausa share her nostalgic story with us. Sandy, husband Joe and their Jo-San kennel have remained true to the Akita breed and its history.

Japanese Grand Champion HARU HIME ROM. Japan's gift to the United States.

			Akiho Ch. Azumazakura
		Akiho Ch. Tōun a.k.a. Azumakumo	
			Gyokurei
Akiho Ch. Tensei			
			Ichitaro
		Fumihime	
			Meigyoku
			Tengai
		Yoshitora	
			Fujihime
Otorahikarijo			
			Hataryumaru
		Mutsuhime	
			Kahoru

69

Am/Can Ch. GOLDEN SUN SEAWOOD WA WA "L" WILAC, ROM.

```
                              Am/Mex, Int'l. C.A.C.I.B., CH. Gin-Gin's Haiyaku-Go of
                                 Sakusaku, ROM
                  Ch. Triple K Mo Tai
                              Ch. Triple K Chiyo
   Ch. Kodiak of Autumn Field
                              Ch. Keen Tai-Yo Oni
                  Golden Sun's Yoko
                              Akijikan No Boshoku Kin
                              Cripple Creek's Thor
                  Ch. Keen Tai-Yo Oni
                              Fawn Brown
   Ch. Golden Sun's Taneha
                              Ch. Gin-Gin Haiyaku-Go of Sakusaku, ROM
                  Sakusaku's Lady Lil
                              Sakusaku's Tiger Lily, ROM
```

70

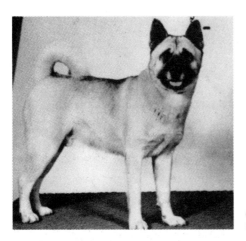

GYOKUSHU OF TOJO KENSHA.
Owned by Kensha Kennels.

THE OUTLOOK

There are hundreds of small kennels in the United States, many of which are producing better than average specimens. Uniformity of type can be seen more frequently, as per the written Standard.

The educational programs of the Akita Club of America and the American Kennel Club will, hopefully, help to produce even more fine results in the years to come.

JAPAN KENNEL CLUB ADDED TO THE AMERICAN KENNEL CLUB'S PRIMARY LIST OF FOREIGN DOG REGISTRY ORGANIZATIONS

New York City, April 13, 1992 - During their April meeting, the Board of Directors of the American Kennel Club approved the addition of the Japan Kennel Club to the AKC's Primary List of Foreign Dog Registry Organizations. This will permit dogs registered with the Japan Kennel Club that are imported into the United States, to be eligible for AKC registration in accordance with the rules and regulations applying to the registration of imported dogs. Individuals (and dogs) suspended prior to the recognition of the Japan Kennel Club will continue to be suspended.

The Japan Kennel Club, established in 1948, is the sole non-profit organization authorized by the Government of Japan as a canine corporation for all-breeds. It is a member of the Federation Cynologique International (FCI) and the Asia Kennel Union (AKU).

The Japan Kennel Club registers more than 250,000 dogs annually which makes it Japan's principal registry and the second largest registry in the world (second only to the American Kennel Club). The Club also holds approximately 500 dog events annually throughout Japan, several of which are internationals shows, and issues several different championship titles.

The governing body for over 950 local member clubs and approximately 100,000 individual members, the Japan Kennel Club's headquarters are located in Tokyo at 1-5, Kanda-Suda-cho, Chiyoda-Ku, Tokyo, 101, Japan.

For further information on the registration of dogs imported from Japan, please write to the American Kennel Club, 5580 Centerview Drive, Suite 200, Raleigh, North Carolina, 27606-3390, Attention: Foreign Registrations.

American Kennel Club News Release: Japan Kennel Club added to the American Kennel Club's primary list of foreign dog registry organizations.

5

The Evolution of the Parent Club Standard

IN ORDER TO UNDERSTAND how today's Akita Standard in America came to be, we must go back to Japan and trace its long and often complex journey, beginning with The Nipponken Hozonkai, or The Society for the Preservation of Japanese Dogs, founded by a select group or committee including Yonikichi Hiraiwa, Shiro Itagaki, Shinichi Komatsu and headed by the esteemed Mr. Hiroshi Saito. It was these gentlemen who had the critical act of saving the Japanese native dogs known as "Nippon Inu."

Hiroshi Saito's efforts were rewarded in June 1928 by the formality of the acceptance by the public of this worthy organization. On November 3, 1934, a national holiday, when Japan commemorated the late Great Emperor Meiji, no fewer than 100 Nippon Inu joined the happy throng of people in a parade.

JAPANESE STANDARDS

To aid those who would propagate these native breeds, a deep study by those experts involved in the recognition of these worthy animals produced a Standard. It was entitled "The Standard Points of the Nippon-Inu," as adopted by the Nippon-Inu Hozonkai.

The Standard Points of the "Nippon-Inu" Adopted by the Nippon-Inu Hozonkai

1. MEDIUM SIZE

Nature and Expression—Sharp and fierce, with good-natured simplicity and excellent scenting power. The whole behaviour shows liveliness. Gait brisk and smart.

General Appearance—Well-balanced body. Sex features distinct. Frame well knit. Muscles well developed. Shoulder height and length of body in males 50–59 cm.; in females 47–53 cm. The proportion of shoulder height to length of body is 100–110 in males; in females the latter gains slightly.

Ears—Small and triangular. Stand erect, tapering, bending forward slightly.

Eyes—Rather triangular. The outer canthus higher. Iris dark brown.

Muzzle—Bridge of nose straight, and peak pointed. Muzzle stout and firm. Lips compressed and thin.

Head and Neck—High-browed. Cheeks well developed. Powerful neck.

Forelegs—Shoulder blades well developed. Hocks straight and toes tightly closed.

Hind Legs—Muscular and straight, with strong hock joints.

Chest—Deep. Ribs moderately sprung. Breast well developed.

Back—Straight.

Tail—Massive and powerful; straight or curled; long enough to reach the hock.

Loins—Strong.

Coat—Uppercoat stiff and straight. Undercoat soft and thick. The hair on the tail long and bushy.

Colour—The colour may be either fawn, white, wheaten, black, brindle, brownish grey, cinder-grey, iron-grey, silver-grey or black and tan.

Disqualifications
1. *All the aforesaid characteristics should be distinct.*
2. *Overshot or undershot.*
3. *Hereditary short-tail.*
4. *Ears not erect, except in pups.*

Deductions
1. *Any deformation caused by injury.*
2. *Undernourishment.*
3. *Pink or butterfly nose.*
4. *Black and white, or brown and white coat.*

N.B. a) *With "army-dogs" the coat should preferably be of any other colour but pure white.*
b) *Spurs preferably should be removed.*

2. LARGE SIZE
(Only the points different from those of the medium size are noted.)

Nature and Expression—Sharp and fierce, with good-natured simplicity. The whole behaviour should be preferably grave.

General Appearance—Sex features distinct. Well-balanced body. Frame firm and sturdy. Muscles well developed. Shoulder height in males 62–73 cm.; in females 57.5–65 cm. The proportion of shoulder height to length of body is 100–110; in females the latter gains slightly.

Tail—Massive and powerful; straight or curled; long enough to reach the hock.

Deduction.
Tail which is not curled.

3. SMALL SIZE
(Only the points different from those of the medium size are noted.)

General Appearance—Sex features distinct. Well-balanced body. Frame well knit. Muscles well developed. The proportion of shoulder height to length of body is 100–110; in females the latter gains slightly. Shoulder height in males 38–42.5 cm.; in females 35–39.5 cm.

Tail—Thick and strong. Those long enough to reach the hock should be straight or curled. Short ones should bear the resemblance of bob tails, but not quite the same.

N.B. In the small size only, hereditary short tail is not disqualified.

To use the Standard is remarkably simple. The *medium size text* is the main body. To find the original Standard for the Odate Dog or Akita Dog, use the medium text and add on the fine points of the *large size* text.

To find, for example, the Standard for the Shiba dog, use the medium text and add on the *small size* text.

This is the same text that was published in the January 1, 1936, American Kennel Club *Gazette*.

It can easily be seen that the native breeds had, and kept, a remarkable similarity to this day.

Today's modern Standard for the Japanese *large size* breed, the Akita, as presented to the Japan Kennel Club by the Nihon-ken Hozonkai (NIPPO), October 30, 1992, is as follows:

Standards for the Japanese Large Size Breed (Akita)

The Nihon-Ken Hozonkai (NIPPO)

1. Nature and Expression

The dog possesses an intrepid spirit whilst being loyal and self-possessed.
There is sophistication in its good-natured simplicity. The appearance should be dignified.

2. General Appearance

Sex features should be distinct. The body should be well balanced with a sturdy bone structure and well-developed muscles. Males should have a height to length ratio of 100:110. The female has a somewhat longer body.
The height for males is 67 cm. and for females 61 cm., with the acceptable range being 3 cm. either upwards or downwards.

3. Ears

Small and triangular, angled slightly forward but standing firm and erect.

4. Eyes

Somewhat triangular and slanted upwards. The color of the iris should be a dark liver-brown.

5. Muzzle

The bridge of the nose should be straight. The mouth should be firm and steady, the nostrils should be tight.

The lips should be drawn firmly when closed. Teeth should be strong and the bite correct.

6. Head and Neck
The forehead should be broad. The neck should be well-developed, but thick and powerful.

7. Forelegs
The shoulder blades should be well developed, with proper angulation. The legs should extend straight down with the paws giving the appearance of a tight grip.

8. Hind legs
The hind legs should have spring and yet should maintain a solid stance. The hock joints should be resilient and the paws should give the appearance of a tight grip.

9. Chest
The chest should be deep, the ribs well sprung, and the breast well developed.

10. Back and Loin
The back should be straight and the loins stout and powerful.

11. Tail
The tail should be thick, powerful, and curled, the full length of which should reach almost to the hock joint.

12. Coat
The overcoat should be straight and harsh.

The undercoat should be dense and soft. The hair on the tail should be somewhat longer than the body hair and should stand off. Coat color should be brindle (sesame), red, black, tiger-brindle, or white. Color and quality should have the typical characteristics of the Japanese breeds.

Deductions
1. Any acquired deformations and signs of inappropriate nourishment.
2. Nose color unsuitable for particular coat color.
3. Spots, speckles, or patches of color on coat.

Disqualifications
1. Lack of typical characteristics of the Japanese breeds.
2. Overshot or undershot.
3. Congenital short tail.
4. Tail with no curl.

Note
Dewclaws should preferably be removed.

Supplement
1. **Tail types**
   (1) Sickle tail
       (Disqualification in case of large size breed)
   (2) Curled tail
       (Drum curl, tight curl, left curl, double curl)

2. **Coat Colors**
   (1) Brindle (Sesame)
       Brindle (Sesame)

White brindle (White sesame)	(2) Red
	Red
—Black hairs mingled into a white coat	Light red
	Crimson
Red brindle (Red sesame)	(3) Black
	(4) Tiger brindle
—Black hairs mingled into a red coat	Tiger brindle
	Red tiger brindle—
Black brindle (Black sesame)	Black on red base
	Black tiger brindle—
—Black hairs mingled into a grey-black coat	Black on grey-black
	(5) White

The Japan Kennel Club, in turn, now uses the following Standard for its judges.

Akita

General Appearance and Characteristics

Large-sized dog sturdily built, well balanced and with much substance, secondary *sex characteristics strongly marked, with high nobility and dignity in a naive feeling, and the constitution tough.* The ratio of height at withers to length of body is 10:11, *but the length of body of bitches slightly longer than dogs.* The temperament is *composed, faithful,* docile and *keen in sense.* (SIZE) Height: Dogs 67 cm., bitches *61 cm.* There is a tolerance of 3 cm. shorter or taller.

Head

The size of skull *balances with body,* and the forehead broad, with defined stop and clear furrow, *but no wrinkle.* The cheeks moderately developed, the nasal bridge straight, with large and black nose. In case of white coat, flesh color permitted. The muzzle moderately long and strong *with base thick and tip thin but not pointed,* and the teeth strong with scissors bite. The lips tight. (EYES) Relatively small, *almost* triangular, set *moderately* apart, dark brown in color and a darker color desirable. (EARS) Relatively small, thick, slightly rounded at tips, triangular, set moderately apart, inclining forward and pricked.

Neck

Thick and muscular, *without dewlap,* in balance with head.

Body
The back straight and *strong*, and the loins broad and muscular. The chest deep, forechest well developed, the ribs moderately *well* sprung and belly well drawn up.

Tail
Set on high, thick and carried vigorously curled over back, and the tip nearly reaching hocks when let down.

Forequarters and Hindquarters
The shoulders moderately sloping and developed, the forearms straight and heavy boned, and the elbows *tight well. The hind legs well developed, strong and moderately angulated.* (FEET) Thick, round, *well closed tightly and arched.*

Gait
Resilient and powerful gait.

Coat
The outer coat harsh and straight, undercoat soft and dense, *the withers and rump covered with slightly longer hair, and the hair on tail longer than on the rest.* (COLOR) Red, *tiger brindle, sesame* and white. *All the above-mentioned colors except white must have "URAJIRO."**

Faults
(DISQUALIFICATIONS)
1. Cryptorchid
2. Ears not pricked
3. Hanging tail
4. *Long hair (shaggy)*

(FAULTS)
1. *Marking (white background)*
2. *Black mask*
3. Shyness
4. *Extreme* malocclusion
5. *Short tail*
6. Spotted tongue
7. *Bitchy dogs/Doggy bitches*
8. *Irises* light in color
9. *Missing* teeth

*(URAJIRO: Whitish coat on the sides of the muzzle and on the cheeks, on the underside of the jaw and neck and on the chest and stomach, and the underside of the tail, and on the inside of the legs.)

Long-haired or coated Akita puppies.

(Author's Note: The translation is not the best, in our opinion. At this point, mention should be made of the historical summary and Standard used by the Fédération Cynologique Internationale [FCI] on the Akita. So many glaring errors have been found in the text of this document that we cannot give it a critique.)

Another registering body of interest in Japan is that of the Akitainu Kyokai organization (AKIKYO), established in 1948. This registry includes the Akita among other native breeds. The last revised Standard for the Akita to guide judges and breeders was adopted June 1, 1989. This was an update from the March 20, 1949, and December 10, 1954, revisions. As a simple guideline, this Standard will suffice, but in no way does it compare to the explicitness of the document of the Akita Dog Preservation Society of Japan that will follow.

The Standard of the Akita Dog as put forth by the largest Akita club in Japan today, the Akitainu Hozonkai (AKIHO), established in 1927, should interest us deeply. The AKIHO's members are dedicated students of the breed, and this Standard clearly enables us to see how the Akita has been preserved and

80

improved in Japan over the years. It was also this Standard that aided the American Akita Club Standard committee, prior to AKC recognition, with their final Standard submitted to the American Kennel Club.

The Standard printed here is comparatively brief. It is accompanied by an in-depth English translation done by Walter Imai, past chairman of AKIHO, Los Angeles Branch. Mr. Imai's expertise as a translator stems from eleven years of formal schooling. Of those few translations made from Japanese to English, this translation by Walter Imai, with extensive research, has proven to be the most accurate.

AKITAINU STANDARD
Adopted September 18, 1955

CHARACTERISTICS

An Akita is quiet, strong, dignified and courageous. He is also loyal and respectful, reserved and noble. He is sensitive and deliberate yet possesses quickness.

OVERALL BODY STRUCTURE

The body is well balanced with a sturdy bone structure and well-developed tendons and ligaments, while the skin is free of wrinkles. Differences in sex should be readily apparent through general appearance. In the dog (male) the ratio of height to body length is 100 to 110. The bitch is slightly longer in length. The height of the dog is 26¼ inches while the height of the bitch is 23⅞ inches, plus or minus 1⅛ inches. The ratio of the height of the depth of the chest is 2 to 1.

HEAD

The skull is large and a little flat at the top. Its forehead is wide without wrinkles but has a definite longitudinal crease. There is a well-proportioned *stop* (depression between the cranial and nasal bones) between the forehead and the muzzle. The cheeks are full.

NECK

The neck is thick and powerful. The skin around the neck is free of wrinkles and the coat appropriately bristled.

EAR

The ears are thick, rather small, triangular in shape, and tilt slightly forward. The lines are straight and the ears stand erect. The distance between the ears is not narrow but not too wide.

EYES

The shape of the eye is approximately triangular. They are deep-set and slightly slanted. The eye rims are dark brownish in color. The distance between the eyes is proportionate.

MUZZLE (Mouth and Nose)

The nose (black portion) is full and the ridge straight. The base of the mouth is wide, the frontal portion not pointed and the lips drawn. The whiskered region is full.

TEETH

The teeth are strong and have a scissor bite.

CHEST AND STOMACH

The chest is broad. The rib cage is full. The forechest is well developed and defined. The stomach is drawn without flabbiness (tucked up).

BACK AND HIP

The back is straight and the hip is powerful.

FORELEGS (Arms)

The shoulders are well developed with proper shoulder angulation. The elbows (joint) are strong. The upper forelegs are straight, strong and thick. The *pasterns* (portion directly above paws) are slightly slanted. The paws are round, large, and thick, and have a firm grip.

HIND LEGS

The hind legs are well developed, springy, powerful and sturdy. The rear pasterns have proper angles and possess a strong kick or thrust. The paws are thick with a strong grip.

TAIL

The tail is thick and tightly wound. The length of the tail when extended must reach the hock joint. The types of curls are called right curl, left curl, single straight and double curl.

COAT

The outercoat is coarse and straight, while the undercoat is fine and thick. The coat at the withers (shoulder region) and rump is slightly longer than the rest of the body. The tail has the longest coat.

COLOR OF COATS: White, black, red, silver-tipped, brindle and pinto.

MINOR FAULTS
1. Permanent injury and dietary deficiency.
2. Color of coat unbecoming to an Akita.
3. Undesirable color combination of coat and eye rim.
4. Loss of tooth or teeth. Undershot and overshot jaws.
5. Black spotting on tongue.
6. Lacking in courage, being timid or displaying ferociousness, or otherwise lacking the qualities suitable for Akitas.

MAJOR FAULTS
1. Floppy ears by birth (ears failing to stand).
2. Straight tail by birth.
3. Excessively long or short coat.
4. Color of nose not matching the color of coat. (Reddish or pink nose acceptable with white coat.)
5. Bilateral or unilateral cryptorchidism.
6. Other defects detracting from the qualities of Akitas.

AN ANALYSIS OF THE AKITAINU HOZONKAI STANDARD FOR THE AKITA

(Written by the research committee of the Akitainu Standard in Japan, with the use of historical records. Translated from the Japanese by Walter Imai, chairman, Akitainu Hozonkai, Los Angeles Branch.)

INTRODUCTION: THE AKITA CHARACTER

The term "character," as applied to an animal, is not easy to define. Our analysis of the Akita's character is traditional and historical, drawn from what has been passed on to us from the older generation, and from our own experiences with the breed, as well as from written material and literature from years past.

An Akita has quiet strength, dignity and courage. An Akita is large, with a powerful bone structure as the foundation of the body. The dog's sheer size, combined with its regal bearing, gives it the aura of being "king of all dogs."

An Akita's nature is to be intensely loyal to its master. This is especially strong in the Akita compared to other breeds. This characteristic parallels the intensely loyal character of the traditional Japanese people.

An Akita's outward appearance, reflecting the inner nature, is calm but at the same time very brave. While the Akita does not challenge first, neither does it back down from the challenge of another.

The character is not an aspect of the Akita that we can measure with a yardstick. Nevertheless it is a fundamental and most important aspect of the breed. Call it what you will—class, pride, bearing—it must be present for a dog to be a good Akita.

A. OVERALL STRUCTURE

The structure of the body governs the capabilities of the Akita. The structure is seen by examining the dog's basic parts and organs and its basic movements. It involves the height, length, weight and general appearance of the dog.

The bone structure must be powerful, tight and well balanced. Muscles, tendons and ligaments must be well developed and strong. Such development must be accompanied by natural beauty. If an Akita does not possess a well-developed structure, the dog is sloppy, loose-jointed, without balance and physically weak.

The torso is divided into the front section, the midsection and the hind section. If the proportions of these sections are not proper, the Akita in its standing position will not look right because it will not have the balance that it requires. Furthermore, its movements will not be smooth, and therefore the dog will not possess staying power. The proper proportions of the sections determine the balance of the structure of the torso.

The location of the front, mid- and hind sections is as follows: Looking at the dog's profile in a normal standing posture, the front section extends from the front of the chest or brisket to an imaginary vertical line drawn through the point of the elbow. The midsection extends from this line to another imaginary vertical line drawn through the point where the dog's hind leg intersects with the body. The hind section extends from this second vertical line to the back of the haunch.

1. The ratio of the torso sections to each other in length: (front) 1 to (mid-) 1.4 to (hind) 1.

2. Depth of chest is 55 percent of the height of the dog. Example: at the ideal height of 66.7 centimeters (26¼ inches), the depth of chest should ideally be 36.9 cm. (14½ in.), or between an upper limit of 37 cm. (14½ in.) and a lower limit of 33.4 cm. (13¼ in.).

3. Chest circumference is 23 percent greater than the height of the dog. Example: At the ideal height of 66.7 cm., circumference of the chest should ideally be 81.8 cm. (32¼ in.), or between an upper limit of 84.8 cm. (33½ in.) and a lower limit of 78.8 cm. (31 in.).

4. Width of the chest is 44 percent as great as the height of the dog. Example: At the ideal height of 66.7 cm., width of the chest should ideally be 29 cm. (11½ in.), or between an upper limit of 30.7 cm. (12 in.) and a lower limit of 28.1 cm. (11 in.).

5. Width of the hips is 40 percent as great as the height of the dog. Example: At the ideal height of 66.7 cm., width through the hips should ideally be 27 cm. (10½ in.), or between an upper limit of 28 cm. (11 in.) and a lower limit of 25.3 cm. (10 in.).

6. Weight: At the ideal height of 66.7 cm. (26¼ in.), the Akita should ideally weigh 45 kilograms (99 pounds).

(*Author's note*: Measurements are rounded off to the nearest ¼ inch. Those who wish may make their own conversions from the more precise metric units given. Divide centimeters by 2.54 to get inches. Multiply kilograms by 2.2 to get pounds.)

The relationship of the depth of chest and the stomach is as follows: The chest and the stomach form a gentle curve, with the stomach severely tucked up toward the hips.

The relationship of body length to back and hip is as follows: The back is the portion of the topline between the shoulder blade and the loin. The length of the back is one-third the length of the body and should be level. Example: At the ideal length of body of 79.86 cm. (31½ in.), the back should measure 23.96 cm. (9½ in.).

The ratio of height of dog to depth of chest called for in the Standard is two to one. However, because the desirable cross section of the chest is rather triangular in shape, it is best to have a somewhat deeper chest, thus the statement that depth of chest is 55 percent of the height of the dog. An Akita with a short back would have a deeper chest and wider shoulders, and the cross section of the chest would be rather round in shape.

The height, depth of chest and all other measurements of the bitch are less than those of the dog.

B. THE WITHERS

The withers is the area that connects the neck with the shoulder blade, the shoulder and the chest. There is a slight indentation where the withers joins the back. An Akita with a high base of neck will have a weak back. A low base, on the other hand, will give a powerful back but impeded movement of the front legs.

C. THE LEGS

The legs support the body of the Akita. Because they must initiate, generate and withstand the shock that the movements create, they must be powerfully constructed and at the same time have much springiness. The cross section of the legs is approximately round. This is necessary for withstanding the various moves and shocks, and for supporting the dog's weight.

D. THE SHOULDER

The shoulder blades form the base of the shoulders. Strong tendons connect the front legs to the front section of the torso at the shoulder blades. The shoulder blade is long and wide and must move freely. It moves back and forth about 10 to 15 degrees. When the Akita is standing naturally, the shoulder blade is at an angle of 55 degrees to the ground.

The longer the shoulder blade, the more it slants, and the shorter it is, the more upright it is. Akitas with long shoulder blades have longer steps, and they are faster.

The shoulder blades should not protrude much from the chest, nor should they recede into it. They should turn neither in nor out.

E. THE UPPER ARM AND FORELEG

The upper arm is constructed of the humerus, which is long in relation to the shoulder blade. It is parallel with the center of the torso. The angulation of the humerus and the shoulder blade is 110 to 120 degrees. If this angulation is less than 110 degrees, the forelegs are drawn back and the chest will protrude. If the humerus is too long, the dog's step will be low, and if it is too short, the step will be high.

From the front, the humerus is perpendicular to the ground.

The forelegs must be parallel, but they should open slightly at the pastern. A vertical line from the point of the shoulder should divide the foreleg approximately in half.

From the side, a vertical line through the withers should barely touch the elbow.

F. PASTERN AND GRIP

The pastern serves to cushion the impact of the dog's movement. If it slants to a large degree, it will not support the dog's weight well, but if it is upright, it will not absorb the shock received by the leg. In either case, the dog's normal movement will be impaired. In the Akita, the proper angulation of the pastern to a line perpendicular to the ground is 10 to 15 degrees.

Also, in the Akita, the grip has been considered very important from years back. The paws should be large, round and thick, without spacing between the toes. The color of the pad should be black. A liver-colored pad indicates lack of pigment in the whole body (lips, eye rims, etc.). The nails should be short and powerful. As in the case of the pad, the nails should be dark in color.

G. HIND LEG

The front legs support the weight of the body and change the direction of movement. The hind legs start and propel the move. Therefore, the upper thigh must be broad and powerful and have strong muscles. The bones—femur, fibula and tibia—are long. The angulation of these bones has been deemed extremely important from the very beginning of the breed. When the dog is standing normally, a vertical line from the back of the rump should touch on the back of the hock joint. The metatarsal bone should be parallel to the same vertical line.

The upper thigh must be full, with strong muscle development. It must be wide, long and thick. The length gives the dog its speed, the width its power. The angle between the pelvic bone and the femur is 80 to 100 degrees. The longer the femur, the more pronounced is the angulation. The more pronounced angulation and the longer bones produce the longer gait. Conversely, the less pronounced angulation would mean a shorter bone and a shorter gait.

The lower thigh is also very important to the movement of the dog. The angulation of the tibia to the femur is 110 to 125 degrees. The fibula and tibia should be supported firmly by ligaments and tendons. The longer the fibula and tibia, the more pronounced is the angulation to the metatarsus, which is normally 140 to 145 degrees.

When the Akita is in a normal standing position, the hock joint as viewed from the rear can be bisected by a vertical line that goes through the point of the rump. Hock joints that turn in or out are faulty.

Viewed from the side, a wide angle of the hock joint (called straight hock) would be weak in generating movement. On the other hand, if the angle is too sharp (called bent hock), the metatarsus is too sharply angled with the ground and cannot support the dog's body weight. In either case, the dog will lack stamina.

H. ANUS

The anus should not protrude, but should be large and tight.

I. TAIL

The tail consists of the trunk of the tail and its hair. It expresses the character of the dog and is also the rudder in the movement of the body. It should be thick, and can be either round or flat. The curl should be powerful and can be carried on the left or right rump or even in a double curl.

88

The *length* of the tail in extended position is specified as reaching the hock joint. However, the position of the hock joint in terms of the height of the dog varies enough so that a more absolute Standard is desirable (the joint has become lower in recent years). Therefore the Akita's tail length should be two-thirds of the body height of the Akita.

Unlike the other Japanese canine breeds, *the Akita has an absolute requirement that the tail be wound*. Furthermore, the shape and type of the tail influence the value and character of the Akita. It is very important that the tail add to the regal bearing and brave character of the Akita. This is especially important today, because the Akita is primarily a show dog.

A tail that is thick would require more than a single curl, as it would lack strength at the tip. However, if a tail is thin, the curl may be shaped well, but the curl itself will be small. On the other hand, a large curl with a thin tail will lack the necessary dignity.

Generally speaking, the tail of a dog is based higher on the back than that of a bitch. This is so because of the dog's more aggressive nature. Furthermore, the hip bone of the bitch is large and is structured in such a way as to make its tail set lower.

J. HEAD

It has been passed on to modern times from years ago that in judging an Akita the structure of the head is important above all, as it houses the brain, which is the origin of all the actions of the dog.

The first requirement is that the *size* of the head be in balance with the size of the body. The size of the head, supported by the neck, influences the center of gravity (the balance) of the Akita. Generally speaking, one of the outstanding features of the Akita compared to the other Japanese breeds (Inu, Shiba, Hokaido Dog, etc.) is that the head is large.

The *shape* of the head from directly above is approximately triangular. The *length* of the head is approximately 9/22 of the height of the body (41 percent). The *thickness* of the head at its largest point is approximately one-half the length of the head.

The *skull* is comprised of the frontal and the rear skulls. The frontal skull (forehead) is wide, and the rear skull (back of the ears) must be well developed, in a way peculiar to the Akita head. An undersized rear skull thus is lacking in one of the distinct features of the Akita.

An old saying in the annals of Akita literature is that "the neck is long and the jaw wide." A short neck is undesirable because it would tend to restrict the dog's movements.

The *forehead* is formed by the frontal skull. It is broad and only slightly rounded. The forehead must be broad because its development is related to the development of the brain.

The *vertical crease* running down the center of the forehead is shallow but must be distinct. An indistinguishable crease or a round forehead without the crease would be considered totally unlike the Akita of past or present.

The *stop* has a direct bearing on the quality of the facial expression. It should be pronounced. The stop is formed by the meeting of the forehead and the bridge of the nose. Viewed from the side, it gives the Akita its distinct appearance and is very important. However, when the stop is too pronounced it will show a more than strong character and even indicate a violent nature. The side view should show the frontal skull and the bridge of the nose to be parallel.

K. THE EYES

The eyes are *approximately triangular* in shape, and they are *deep-set. The eye rim must be dark brown.* The *eyes are slightly slanted.* As it is said of all animals, the eyes express the nature, disposition and feelings of the Akita. The size and position, and the distance between the eyes, are relative to the size of the head.

Together with the stop and the vertical crease, the eyes make up the facial expression of the Akita and are one of the important factors in the overall quality of the breed.

L. THE MOUTH

The mouth is comprised of the upper and lower jaw, including the teeth. Because its function is to chew as well as to bite, it is

90

powerfully constructed and requires some width and depth. When viewed from the side, the line of the mouth forms a 90-degree angle with the front end of the nose. The mouth extends to the corner of the upper jaw, and its width is the width of the muzzle. Although the mouth has to be powerful, it must not be so large or powerful that it detracts from the noble look of the facial features.

M. NOSE

The muzzle starts from the lower part of the forehead and extends to the black portion of the nose. The front part of the nose is large compared to other canine breeds. It is square in shape. Because it possesses the important sense of smell, the nose must be well shaped and tight.

N. THE LIPS

The lips are drawn tightly, paralleling the jaw bones. They should not be flabby, but just full enough to cover the teeth.

O. THE TEETH

Generally speaking, a dog of sturdy bone structure with large paws must have large, powerful teeth. The Akita is no exception. Because in its wild state the Akita had to fight other animals and also maintain good health, it has exceptionally long, sharp and strong teeth compared to the other native Japanese breeds of dog.

The scissor bite is the only acceptable bite. Among the teeth, the four canine teeth especially must be powerful and have proper bite.

P. THE EARS

It is said that if the eyes are the mirror of the heart, the ears are the heart's windows. The noble bearing of the Akita is greatly enhanced by the proper shape, quality and position of the dog's ears.

Like other Japanese purebreds, the Akita has a stand-up ear, showing alertness. When the dog is not feeling well or when it is not up to the occasion, it will flatten its ears.

The quality, shape, position and size of the ears must balance with the size and shape of the head and face. Ears that are too thick give the appearance of insensitivity; therefore, the ears should only be rather thick.

The Standard says the ears must be approximately triangular. The tips should be slightly rounded rather than pointed, indicating the gentleness of the Akita.

As to position of the ear, when viewed from the front as the dog stands erect and looks straight ahead, a vertical line through the tip of the ear must divide the ear equally in half.

The Standard calls for ears "rather small," but here again size must be relative to the size of the head. When folded forward, the tip of the ear should touch the eyelid. Viewed from the front, the highest part of the outer edge of the ear should be in line with the outside corner of the eye. The distance between the tips of the ears is 75 percent of the width of the face.

Q. THE NECK

Because the neck houses the windpipe, the throat must be appropriately thick and long. The skin that covers the neck *must* be tight. The muscles in the neck must be strong and powerful, so that the heavy head is supported for quick and free movement. When the Akita is carrying something in its mouth, the neck must be strong enough to support the weight. In order to properly exercise its sense of smell, the Akita must be able to move its head swiftly. In case of a fight, the neck is the most vulnerable part of the body.

When the neck is long, the shoulder blade tilts more, allowing longer steps and faster movement. However, when the neck is too long, the head cannot be stable, and in general the dog is weaker. Its appearance will also lack dignity.

R. THE COAT

The coat of the Akita has three distinct layers: the outer guard coat, the regular coat and the woolly undercoat.

The *undercoat* is a thick, fine, cottonlike coat. It thins out during the summer months, but it is heavy during the winter to keep the body warm.

The *regular coat* is made of coarse hair, very resilient. The regular coat protects the body from injuries and repels water.

The *outer guard coat* is about 1.5 cm. (½ in.) longer than the regular coat and stands out like needles.

The *whiskers* are permanent; therefore, they are believed to have feeling, unlike the hair of the coat.

The Akita coat must be stiff and *open*. In rain and snow, it should not get soaking wet. If the coat is soft, the body will get completely wet.

THE PRESENT BREED STANDARD

Most imports brought into the United States by returning servicemen and some enterprising souls after World War II were not the best representatives of the breed. Most lacked type, structure, color and, frequently, ideal temperament. Japanese breeders wisely kept the "cream of the crop" for themselves.

Study of the Akita Club of America's Stud Book reveals that until the early '70s few fine specimens were either not used or not used to their potential. Many new Akita owners of the time lacked a thorough knowledge of the heredity of their dogs.

The first Breed Standard, as accepted by the American Kennel Club and proposed by ACA in 1960, specified "A head free from wrinkle," "Coat of almost any color from cream to black" (all-white was omitted), "Neck without excessive dewlap," "Size: Dogs 25½ inches to 27½ inches or more at the shoulder with bitches slightly smaller," "Weight in proportion to size, usually 85 to 110 pounds for dogs, 75 to 90 pounds for bitches." Disqualifying faults were not noted at the end of the Standard.

In 1963, after much study and concern, the Standard Committee submitted a revised "Standard of Perfection" to members of the Akita Club of America, which those present approved. It was better written than the first Standard and contained important additions and deletions. One controversial change was: Height: "Males,

25 inches to 28 inches or more; Bitches, 23 inches to 26 inches or more" with no mention of weight. Colors were specified as "Solids, Brindles, Pintos, Whites." Most important change here was the addition of white. "Solid white dogs may have a liver nose but the black nose is more desirable." Head: ". . . free from wrinkle *when at ease.*" Stop: added to the original "A stop well marked but not abrupt" were the words "The furrow extends well up the forehead." Faults were included as follows:

MINOR—*Undesirable*	MAJOR—*Disqualifying*
a. Round or light eyes	a. Drop or broken ears
b. Excessive dewlap	b. Deafness
c. Dark spots on tongue	c. Uncurled tail
d. Coarseness in bitches	d. Altering length of coat
e. Overrefinement in males	e. Shyness, viciousness or instability
f. Looseness	f. "Pink" eye rims or lips
g. Lack of spirit	g. Butterfly nose

In October 1965, another proposed Standard suggested weight of Akitas should be: "Males—90 to 140 pounds generally; Bitches—70 to 100 pounds generally."

In 1972, much controversy prevailed among Parent Club members regarding the Standard of Perfection for Akitas as it should be written in order to gain recognition for the breed with the American Kennel Club. The question of size, color and the "wrinkle" factor dominated.

On December 12, 1972, the Board of Directors of the American Kennel Club approved the following Standard for Akitas, which became effective April 4, 1973, and as of this writing remains as written although for the past ten years an ACA Standard revision committee has been actively pursuing change for the future.

GENERAL APPEARANCE—Large, powerful, alert, with much substance and heavy bone. The broad head, forming a blunt triangle, with deep muzzle, small eyes and erect ears carried forward in line with back of neck, is characteristic of the breed. The large, curled tail, balancing the broad head, is also characteristic of the breed.

HEAD—Massive but in balance with body; free of wrinkle when at ease. Skull flat between ears and broad; jaws square and powerful with minimal dewlap. Head forms a blunt triangle when viewed from above. Fault—Narrow or snipy head.

Muzzle—Broad and full. Distance from nose to stop is to distance from stop to occiput as 2 is to 3. *Stop*—Well defined, but not too abrupt. A shallow furrow extends well up forehead.

Nose—Broad and black. Liver permitted on white Akitas, but black always preferred. Disqualification—Butterfly nose or total lack of pigmentation on nose.

Ears—The ears of the Akita are characteristic of the breed. They are strongly erect and small in relation to rest of head. If ear is folded forward for measuring length, tip will touch upper eye rim. Ears are triangular, slightly rounded at tip, wide at base, set wide on head but not too low and carried slightly forward over eyes in line with back of neck. Disqualification—Drop or broken ears.

Eyes—Dark brown, small, deep-set and triangular in shape. Eye rims black and tight.

Lips and Tongue—Lips black and not pendulous; tongue pink.

Teeth—Strong with scissors bite preferred, but level bite acceptable. Disqualification—Noticeably undershot or overshot.

NECK AND BODY

Neck—Thick and muscular; comparatively short, widening gradually toward shoulders. A pronounced crest blends in with base of skull.

Body—Longer than high, as 10 is to 9 in males; 11 to 9 in bitches. Chest wide and deep; depth of chest is one-half height of dog at shoulder. Ribs well sprung, brisket well developed. Level back with firmly muscled loin and moderate tuck-up. Skin pliant but not loose. *Serious Faults*—Light bone, rangy body.

TAIL—Large and full, set high and carried over back or against flank in a three-quarter, full or double curl, always dipping to or below level of back. On a three-quarter curl, tip drops well down flank. Root large and strong. Tail bone reaches hock when let down. Hair coarse, straight and full, with no appearance of a plume. *Disqualification*—Sickle or uncurled tail.

FOREQUARTERS AND HINDQUARTERS

Forequarters—Shoulders strong and powerful with moderate layback. Forelegs heavy-boned and straight as viewed from front. Angle of pastern 15 degrees forward from vertical. *Faults*—Elbows in or out, loose shoulders.

Hindquarters—Width, muscular development and comparable to forequarters. Upper thighs well developed. Stifle moderately bent and hocks well let down, turning neither in nor out.

Dewclaws—On front legs generally not removed; dewclaws on hind legs generally removed.

Feet—Cat feet, well knuckled up with thick pads. Feet straight ahead.

COAT—Double-coated. Undercoat thick, soft, dense and shorter than outer coat. Outercoat straight, harsh and standing somewhat off body. Hair on head, legs and ears short. Length of hair at withers and rump approximately 2 inches, which is slightly longer than on rest of body, except tail, where coat is longest and most profuse. The occasional long-hair Akita puppy can be placed in a proper pet home, or if chosen, eliminated IF the breeder is sure it is a long coat, and if he/she has the ability to do so. One should breed away from coats that do not conform to the breed Standard. *Fault*—Any indication of ruff or feathering.

COLOR—Any color including white, brindle or pinto. Colors are brilliant and clear and markings are well balanced, with or without mask or blaze. White Akitas have no mask. Pinto has a white background with large, evenly placed patches covering head and more than one-third of body. Undercoat may be a different color from outer coat.

96

GAIT—Brisk and powerful with strides of moderate length. Back remains strong, firm and level. Rear legs move in line with front legs.

SIZE—Males 26 to 28 inches at the withers; bitches 24 to 26 inches. Disqualification—Dogs under 25 inches; bitches under 23 inches.

TEMPERAMENT—Alert and responsive, dignified and courageous. Aggressive toward other dogs.

DISQUALIFICATIONS

Butterfly nose or total lack of pigmentation on nose.
Drop or broken ears.
Noticeably undershot or overshot.
Sickle or uncurled tail.
Dogs under 25 inches; bitches under 23 inches.

Approved December 12, 1972

IN CONCLUSION

By perusing the various differences in all of the Akita Standards presented here, it is easy to see that there have been many changes over the years.

Akita breeders carry the responsibility of a unified and correct interpretation of the Standard as it exists in their country.

Parts of the Akita

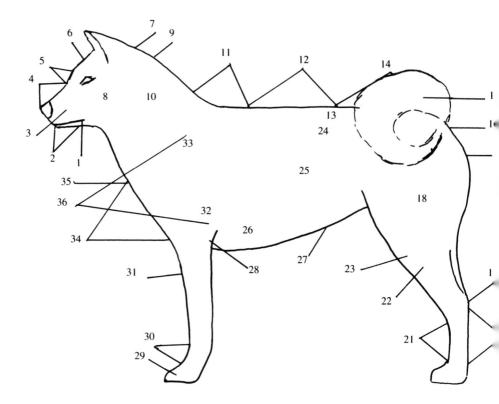

1. flew	14. croup	26. chest
2. lower jaw	15. tail	27. abdomen
3. muzzle	16. tailset	28. elbow
4. foreface	17. point of haunch	29. paws
5. stop	18. thigh	30. pastern
6. skull	19. point of hock	31. forearm
7. occiput	20. hock	32. upper arm
8. cheek	21. metatarsus	33. shoulder blade
9. crest of neck	22. lower thigh	34. fore chest
10. neck	23. point of stifle	35. breast bone or
11. withers	(knee)	prosternum
12. back	24. loin	36. shoulder
13. hip	25. ribs	

6

An Analysis of the Akita—As It Stands

PROPORTION

The male dog's height to body length ratio is 100 to 110. The bitch is a trifle longer in length.

HEAD

"An Akita's head is a symphony of triangles."
—Joan Linderman in *Kennel Review*

Although the head is in balance with the body, it is large in appearance. The wide, slightly rounded forehead has no wrinkles. Two important traits not to be overlooked are the distinct vertical crease down the center of the forehead and the full, full cheeks. The nose should be large, black and pretty much square-shaped. It should be a healthy nose. The white Akita may have a liver-colored nose. A dog's head should show masculinity; the bitch's, femininity.

EARS

The stand-up ear is fairly small and triangular in shape. It is broad at the base, slightly rounded at the tip and thick enough not to show weakness. The inner part of the ear is sheltered by the forward (45-degree) angle or tilt over the eyes.

Because ears are a distinguishing characteristic, they are extremely important.

EYES

Deep-set, dark brown color and almost triangular in shape. They are slightly slanted. The eye rims are dark and tight. There must be no sagging of the lower rim. This is a stressed characteristic. Breeders and judges must adhere to a correct eye.

MOUTH

Powerful in structure with tight black lips and large, powerful teeth in a proper scissor bite is to be preferred. All four canine teeth should be present. Preference is to no black spots on the tongue.

NECK

Tightly covered by skin, it must be well muscled and not too short. Proper length of neck must be present for the head to move swiftly.

BODY

Powerful, tight and well balanced. The back, or topline, must be level. The chest is dropped when viewed from the side but actually looks higher when viewed from the front. The loin must be well tucked-up.

TAIL

The tail's trunk is thick, the root strong. The Akita must have a curled or wound tail. We cannot stress this enough. The balance, the dignity and the character of the breed depend on the tail's correct carriage. If pulled down the tail should reach the hock.

ANUS

Because of the Akita's curled tail, the anus is in an area more visible than on a drop tail breed. It should never protrude, should be fairly large, dark in color and tight.

LEGS AND FEET

The legs must be muscular, well developed and show power when moving. In the forelegs there must be no hint of the elbows going in or out. In the hindquarters, the hock should turn neither in nor out. The stifle should be only moderately bent.

The feet are large and round. Thick pads and no indication of space between the toes are desired.

COMMENT

Some words in the American Standard for Akita dogs are: alert, responsive, dignified, courageous, aggressive toward other dogs. Only an Akita with a well-wound tail and an alert forward ear set could define these words.

SUMMARY

The Japanese Akita male is a squarely built, powerful, masculine-appearing dog. His well-developed, free-of-wrinkle head is full cheeked with a distinct vertical crease running down the center of

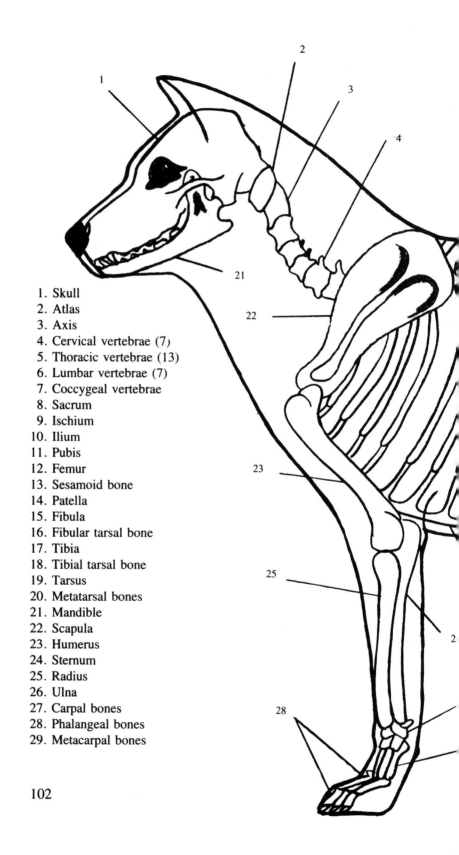

1. Skull
2. Atlas
3. Axis
4. Cervical vertebrae (7)
5. Thoracic vertebrae (13)
6. Lumbar vertebrae (7)
7. Coccygeal vertebrae
8. Sacrum
9. Ischium
10. Ilium
11. Pubis
12. Femur
13. Sesamoid bone
14. Patella
15. Fibula
16. Fibular tarsal bone
17. Tibia
18. Tibial tarsal bone
19. Tarsus
20. Metatarsal bones
21. Mandible
22. Scapula
23. Humerus
24. Sternum
25. Radius
26. Ulna
27. Carpal bones
28. Phalangeal bones
29. Metacarpal bones

102

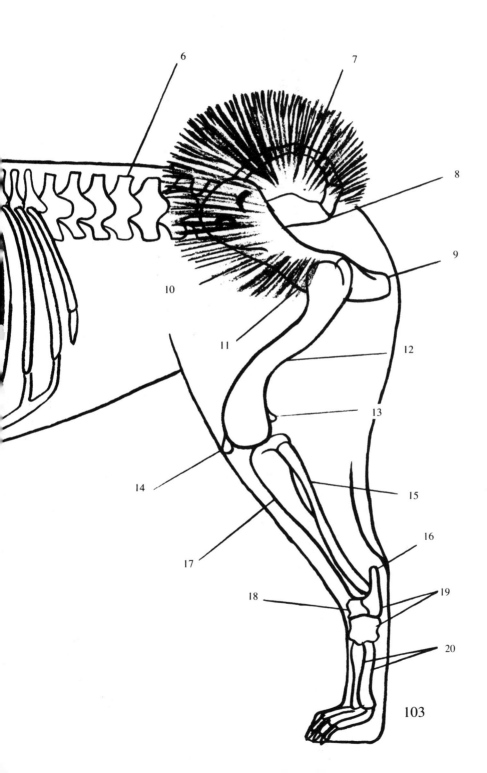

6

7

8

9

10

11

12

13

14

15

16

17

18

19

20

103

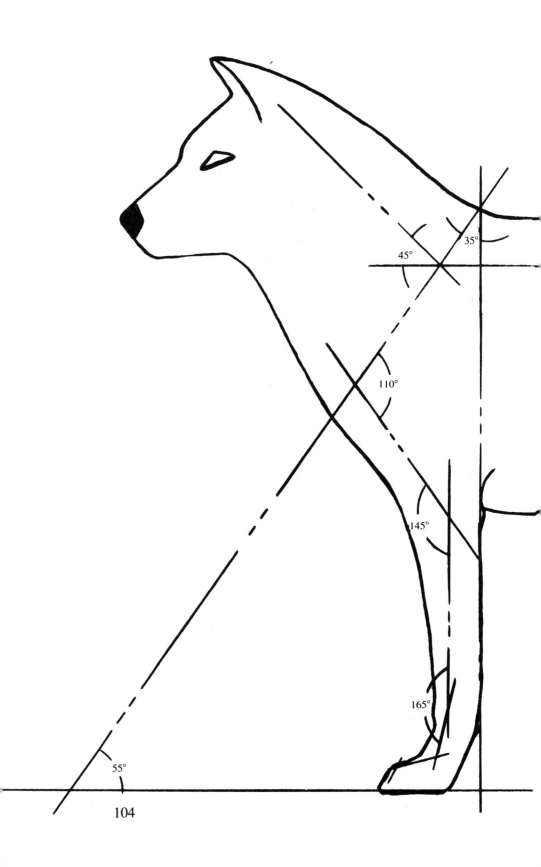

35°

45°

110°

145°

165°

55°

104

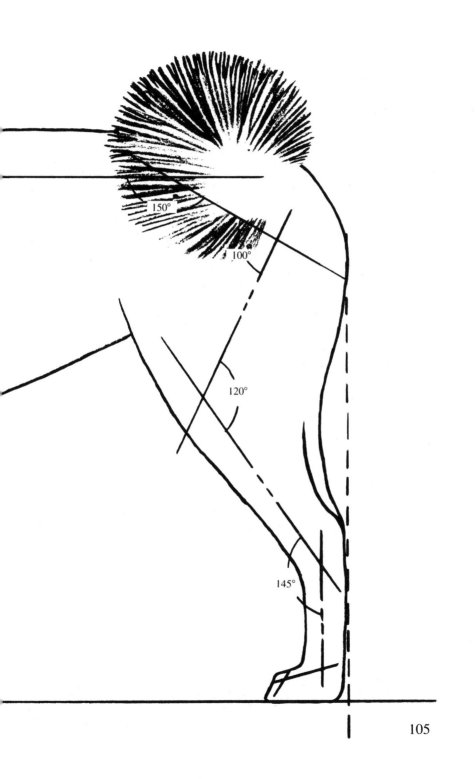

150°

100°

120°

145°

105

the forehead. Dark, triangularly shaped eyes complement the small, stand-up triangular shaped ears that angle forward. The firmly curled tail is a distinguishing characteristic of the breed. Woolly undercoat, coarse outercoat and harsh, bristled guard hairs protect the body. The stand-off coat is vivid in color and the whiskers are permanent.

The female Akita, although showing like physical characteristics, is slightly longer in body, smaller in size and feminine in appearance and nature.

7

The Importance
of Color

In JAPAN'S EARLY DAYS, Japanese dogs were primarily used for hunting and fighting. *Performance had priority over color*. It was not until the establishment of registration bureaus, whose primary function was and is to preserve purebreds and strive for ideal Standards, that color became a major concern and remains so today.

Because a large percentage of Japan's Akitas are shown, and a lesser but sufficiently large enough number are seen in show rings in the United States, we feel the importance of color warrants a place in this book.

WHAT IMPACT DOES COLOR HAVE IN THE SHOW RING?

A dog lacking a vivid and acceptable coat color in Japan very often does not rank high in the show ring, no matter how excellent are the facial features, body type or coat quality. Dull, lackluster colors do not do justice to the elegance of the Akita breed, nor do they adhere to the Standard as it is written.

The learned Mr. Naoto Kajiwara, noted Akita authority, in an article on color in the *Aiken Journal*, Japan, translated by Mr. Tatsuo Kimura, had this to say:

> With the exception of the white coat, the Akita dog's coat color undergoes changes with growth and development. This also adds to the difficulty of judging the true coat color. In the final analysis, one should become capable of judging what he considers to be the appropriate color for each stage of growth. Needless to say, one should consider the color hue admired by the Japanese in the native dog that inhabited the Tohoku region from ancient times. That is, color hues that blend with the elegantly pure Japanese paintings, pristine and refined Japanese antique art objects and the simple but sturdy and strong Japanese architecture should be considered. Otherwise, I believe that one could not possibly come to appreciate the feeling for that simplicity without adornment called "shibusa" or "soboku" so often expressed by the Japanese.

After World War II, Pinto, Aka Goma (red sesame), Brindle and Kurogoma (black sesame) were the most popular colors in Japan. Today, reds, good whites and black-and-white brindle are being shown frequently. The Kurogoma color has disappeared, it is said, in order to eliminate such undesirable features as loose skin and wrinkles, for instance, which seemed to go with that particular color.

The Pinto or "Buchi" coat pattern varies greatly and is now seen less frequently in Japan than in its heyday in the 1950s. According to Mr. Kajiwara, "Perhaps this may reflect the preference for Akita dogs with the quality of simple dignity without gaudiness."

THE AKC STANDARD ON COLOR

The AKC Standard has a very wide range of acceptable colors. However, it bears pointing out that the Standard also reads that a "pinto" has a white background with large, *evenly placed patches* covering head and more than *one-third of the body*! Fortunately, the other popular Akita coat colors usually do adhere to the Standard.

WHITE: The most desired is a pure white with an almost blueing effect. Dark pigmentation on the eye rims and lips serve as an accent. The nose should be black. Although liver is accepted, the darker the nose the better.

RED: There are many shades of red. The soft coordinating color of the undercoat can change the color of the outer layer. White or black masks are acceptable. The white mask is called hoho-boke by the Japanese. When the Akita has tightly drawn black lips, a large black nose and dark eyes of a triangular shape, there is truly nothing more striking or beautiful than the white mask.

BRINDLE: There are various shades of the tiger-striped Akita. To quote Mr. Kajiwara, "The pepper-and-salt brindle has a lighter shade of black, with the muzzle and limbs having a hue as if some frost had descended upon the earth." In the red-and-black brindle, a strong red is not preferred. Subtlety in color is looked for. A brindle's striping covers the body and may also pattern the face. If the face has stripes instead of a black mask, they should be uniform and not unsightly.

At the Akita Club of America board meeting in February 1972, the color brown was approved as an addition to the list of colors people could use in describing their dogs on the official registration forms. Many people had written to say their Akitas were brown rather than any of the colors mentioned in the registration regulations.

Though the official AKC Standard for Akitas calls for "any color including white," and further states, "Colors are brilliant and clear," we've yet to see a "brilliant and clear" brown. With the exception of the white Akita, most other coat colors become richer and deepen as the dog matures. The undercoat, on all but the white, is usually a softer shade than the outer layer and the guard hairs. However, it should blend in so there is no evidence of dramatic contrast.

IN CONCLUSION

Coat color trends in the breed are often influenced by:

1. A popular stud, prepotent for passing on his color to his offspring.
2. The personal preference of a breeder and/or kennel that produces many dogs.
3. Color fads perpetuated by a winning dog who catches the judge's eyes.

There are color differences in the many Akita Standards listed in this text. It becomes a controversial subject among breeders and judges alike. There is no doubt that color is meaningful at dog shows here and abroad. Therefore, for those who show, its importance should not be overlooked. For those who adhere to the written Standard, color becomes a major factor.

8

The Adaptability
of the Akita

THE LATTER HALF of the nineteenth century was a rugged time in Japanese society. It was during these years that the native Japanese dogs were to gradually begin their transformation to the Akita dog as we know it today.

Because of the isolated northern location and the mountainous and wooded terrain that served as a home for these dogs, a toughness and craftiness, necessary for survival, was instilled in their behavior patterns. These same characteristics can be found in today's Akitas.

It was definitely a world ruled by men in those early days, and as a result war games, hunting and dog fighting were socially accepted as they were in so many other countries. The Akita performed creditably in these insensitive and sometimes cruel activities and became a fixed part of crude recreational sports.

As Japanese society advanced and gradually left behind this unstable era, the Akita flourished from around 1920 until the sadness of World War II, when there was a period of decline for everything, including dogs.

"Tommy," Charles and Joyce Basher's first Akita, shown backpacking in the Wind River Wilderness of Wyoming.

When the war ended, the need for peace and beauty was essential for all involved. Thus, the reconstruction period for the Akita seriously started in Japan. The advent of shows and clubs, a better economy and social change dictated to those enamored with the Akita breed that radical changes should be made, and they were.

Because of changes made abroad and those still being made in the United States, the Akita, with its great versatility, is increasingly enjoyed with today's lifestyles.

OBEDIENCE

In the Beginning

Obedience training for the breed was stressed when the first Akitas were brought into the United States, but few owners were ready to take on what they considered the stubborn nature of the animal.

112

BAMBI, southern California's first therapy dog. A three-year-old fawn owned by Dayon Race, Bambi is the first Akita registered as a therapy dog in southern California. Bambi received her registration in July 1992 through Our Best Friends, San Diego Chapter #103 of Therapy Dogs International. She is shown wearing the standard therapy dog uniform, a red harness. The red heart at the front of the harness is her registration badge. Two pin-on badges on the side of the harness are her in-training and wheelchair symbols.

Marge Rutherford was one of the first Akita owners to spend time training the breed. She was a trainer for Valley Hills Obedience Club in California and put in many long, dedicated hours in service to the Akita. Marge Rutherford had a good pair of hands and a gentle but firm manner. She conducted the first all-Akita conformation handling class in 1963.

The first all-Akita Obedience Trial was held on February 16, 1969, by the Akita Club of America. Twelve Akitas were entered in what was then Sub-Novice and two in Novice. Highest Score in Trial went to a bitch, Akita Tani's Kage Boshi, trained and handled by R. Cunningham Short and owned by Liz Harrell.

At that same time, an outstanding young brindle male, Mex. Ch. Imperial Rikimaru, owned and trained by Dennis McElrath, was proving that there were exceptions to every rule. Although his sire, Mex. Ch. Kinsei Suna Nihon no Taishii, CD, had an Obedience title, that title was earned only by the persistence of his owners, Dr. and Mrs. Joseph Vogl. "Tai" was rather slow in the Obedience ring, but in the conformation ring he perked up considerably. His son, "Riki," was just the opposite. He became the first Akita to win a Utility Dog title and was a joy to behold as he worked.

On the East Coast, Sam and Barbara Mullen and Barbara Miller were deeply interested in Obedience work and were the first to enlist the Akita into Brace competition. In the Midwest in the 1970s, Dr. Neal Pitts and Sharon Tucker Hansen took top honors with their highly trained dogs.

Obedience and the Akita
by Bill Bobrow

The Akita is intelligent and trainable. Each individual dog is different, but for the most part no more difficult to train than the other breeds in the Working Group.

Akita temperament makes them normally an independent breed bonding closely to one person or one family. This may include other family pets. However, it is unlikely that Akitas of a particular sex will get along with other dogs of the same sex when left alone. There are few exceptions to this.

Akitas are usually protective of their family and possessions. Most household training should be aimed at controlling this protectiveness so that the dog will not challenge other animals or people while they are in the vicinity of that Akita's family and friends. This can be accomplished through Obedience training.

Dogs should be properly socialized so that they do not growl around food dishes and are accepting of children. Akitas that attack with little provocation have not been raised properly or are unstable. There is no reason to accept such behavior in Akitas or dogs in general. It should be noted that this is reflective of only a small number of the breed. *In most cases it is caused by irresponsible owners.*

On the whole, Akitas are relatively calm, quiet, willing to

114

Ch. KITA NO UNRYU of Sasahara Kensha was imported into the U.S. in 1992 and is the first import to earn a Companion Dog degree. He was sired by Ise Unryu of Ise Meiwa Kensha × Kiyo of Ebe Kensha. He was bred by Yoshiichi Okayama, owned by Frank Sakayeda and shown by Bill Bobrow.

115

Am/Mex/IABKC CH. NORTHLAND TOSHI MARU TRIPLE K CDX, PCX. Owned by C. Kam, C. Parker and B. Bobrow. "Maru" is a dual purpose Akita, finishing a championship and an Obedience title in short order. Maru is a multiple Group placer and is currently in training for a UD with Bill Bobrow.

please and not resentful of training. One characteristic is that they are rapid learners and normally require relatively few corrections. They react well to short training periods.

Training should begin at an early age, as young as ten or twelve weeks. Training at this age should be based on socialization and exposure, an understanding of the dog/owner relationship, learning the meanings of words and commands and walking on leash.

A slip (choke) collar can be introduced at this early age but should be handled with an understanding of the pup's age. The owner should be aware that proper timing on the quick jerk and release of collar pressure is most important. Puppy kindergarten classes are recommended. The correct use of a leather buckle collar is acceptable on a pup.

Puppy training should enforce the desired behavior but should *not* be overly harsh. Insensitive training that does not demand anything of the puppy will create a stubborn, willful dog. Insensitive training that is too demanding and stretches for long periods of time will break a dog's spirit. Most training sessions need not last more

Am/Mex/IABKC CH. INAKA HONEY BARBARA CDX, PC. Most titled Akita bitch in the history of the breed. Trainier, Bill Bobrow.

than fifteen minutes and need not be done on a daily basis. Generally, training should have a fun-play aspect to it.

Akitas have been successfully trained with and without bait. When bait is used it should be linked to praise and is most effective when used intermittently. Much is made about which training techniques are effective on an Akita. Since many different techniques have proven to be effective, we can only conclude that sensitivity in reading a dog and proper timing are more important than the technique used.

The owner should remember that backyard training will most likely only show results in the backyard. Dogs in general require early exposure to all environments where they may be asked to behave. A good Obedience class is a necessity for an obedient Akita. Such a class will teach basic behaviors such as on- and off-leash Heeling, Sitting, Standing on command, lying Down, prolonged Stays with the owner-handler at a distance and allowing strangers to touch and handle the dog. More important, in a class, these behaviors and responses will be learned in proximity to other people and dogs.

AKC has instituted a Canine Good Citizen (CGC) program that stresses these behaviors and responses along with responsible ownership. Akita owners are urged to earn the CGC Certificate, which is issued to dogs who pass the American Kennel Club Good Citizen Test. Local Akita specialty clubs or all-breed training clubs should be contacted for more information on this program. For your information, a CGC test score sheet is printed in this chapter, and a book on the required skills and the test itself is available: *The Canine Good Citizen—Every Dog Can Be One* by Jack and Wendy Volhard (Howell Book House).

When looking for a trainer, it is best to find someone with successful experience in training Akitas or other large, protective breeds. *Find a trainer who likes the breed.* View the trainer's class and try to assess the quality of the graduates. Discuss training with people who have *successfully* trained one or preferably more dogs. Don't be misled by those who say Akitas are not trainable. With few exceptions, people who say such things usually have not trained any breed of dog successfully.

Over 600 Akitas have earned Companion Dog titles from the

American Kennel Club. A large percentage of these have performed most admirably in Obedience competition. In 1990, a study of Akita performance in AKC competition was conducted. Although relatively few Akitas compete in these events, the results were pleasantly surprising.

First Akita Utility Dog. Mex. Ch. Imperial Rikimaru, U.D. Born 4/23/66.

Date: _____ Dog/Number: _____

Club or Organization: _____

Breed: _____

TEST	Pass	Fail
1. Accepting a Friendly Stranger	☐	☐
This test demonstrates that the dog will allow a friendly stranger to approach it and speak to the handler in a natural, everyday situation. The evaluator and handler shake hands and exchange pleasantries. The dog must show no sign of resentment or shyness and must not break position or try to go to the evaluator.		
2. Sitting Politely for Petting	☐	☐
This test demonstrates that the dog will allow a friendly stranger to touch it while it is out with its handler. The evaluator pets the dog and then circles the dog and handler. The dog must not show shyness or resentment.		
3. Appearance and Grooming	☐	☐
This practical test demonstrates that the dog will welcome being groomed and examined and will permit a stranger to do so. It also demonstrates the owner's care, concern and responsibility. The evaluator inspects the dog, then combs or brushes the dog and lightly examines the ears and each front foot.		
4. Out for a Walk (Walking on a loose leash)	☐	☐
This test demonstrates that the handler is in control of the dog. The evaluator may use a pre-plotted course or may direct the handler/dog team by issuing instructions or commands. There must be a left turn, a right turn and an about turn, with at least one stop in between and another at the end. The dog need not be perfectly aligned with the handler and need not sit when the handler stops.		
5. Walking Through a Crowd	☐	☐
This test demonstrates that the dog can move about politely in pedestrian traffic and is under control in public places. The dog and handler walk around and pass close to several people. The dog may show some interest in the strangers, without appearing overexuberant, shy or resentful.		

The American Kennel Club's Canine Good Citizen Test. Reprinted with the kind permission of the American Kennel Club.

120

TEST	Pass	Fail

6. Sit and Down on Command/Staying in Place

This test demonstrates that the dog has training, will respond to the handler's command to sit and down and will remain in the place commanded by the handler (sit or down position, whichever the handler prefers). The handler may take a reasonable amount of time and use more than one command.

7. Praise/Interaction

This test demonstrates that the dog can be easily calmed following play or praise and can leave the area of this test in a mannerly fashion. The handler may use verbal praise, petting, playing with a toy and/or a favorite trick in the allowed 10 seconds of play, and then must calm the dog for the next test.

8. Reaction to Another Dog

This test demonstrates that the dog can behave politely around other dogs. Two handlers and their dogs approach each other from a distance of about 10 yards, stop, shake hands and exchange pleasantries, and continue on for about 5 yards. The dogs should show no more than a casual interest in each other.

9. Reactions to Distractions

This test demonstrates that the dog is confident at all times when faced with common distracting situations. The dog may express a natural interest and curiosity and may appear slightly startled, but should not panic, try to run away, show aggressiveness or bark.

10. Supervised Isolation

This test demonstrates that a dog can be left alone, if necessary, and will maintain its training and good manners. Evaluators are encouraged to say something like, "Would you like me to watch your dog while you make your call?" to add a touch of reality and accentuate the fact that leaving a dog tied and unsupervised is *not* condoned. The dog will be attached to a 6-foot line for three minutes and does not have to stay in position but should not continually bark, whine, howl, pace unnecessarily or show anything other than mild agitation or nervousness.

REMARKS:

SIGNED: _____
Evaluator

GK9TC2 (3/94)

121

- Sixty-nine Akitas earned a total of 200 qualifying Obedience scores in that year.
- Eighteen different Akitas (26 percent) earned class placements, i.e., they placed first through fourth in competitive Obedience at AKC Trials.
- Ten different Akitas earned qualifying scores in Open and Utility competition.

Soho's Don't Mess with My Tutu, Am. & Can. UD, an Akita owned and trained by Hunt Cleveland, earned forty-three qualifying scores in Open and Utility competition. The sixty-nine Akitas with qualifying scores scored better than 2,202 other dogs in competition which includes all AKC breeds.

The myth persists in many breed circles that Obedience training will ruin a dog for the breed ring. This has been disproven by many champions in all breeds. Dogs with AKC Obedience titles have even gone Best in Show at the famous Westminster Kennel Club. The Akitas with titles in both the breed and Obedience ring are too numerous to mention. The many adverse opinions about training for both breed and Obedience probably reflect more upon the trainers than the breed. Proper training should *improve* a dog's behavior in the breed ring.

Most training problems with Akitas can be avoided by starting training at an early age (three months), working with an experienced trainer, setting long-range goals and having patience. People who wait for a dog to reach ninety pounds of misbehaving muscle before they start formal training will obviously have to invest more work and effort in bringing their dog under control.

An old dog *can* be taught new tricks. Ch. Triple K's Kido, CD, earned his Obedience title at ten years of age. But wise owners will start early, avoid abusive training and guide their puppies into Obedience. Time invested early pays off for a lifetime and strengthens the canine-human bond.

Akita owners who wish to compete in organized Obedience competition will find it a most rewarding experience. It is a way for them to enjoy their pets and meet other animal lovers. The dogs will delight in the bonding, the activities, and the trips to new places. Owner and Akita will benefit in ways too numerous to

CH. TRIPLE K KIDO, CD. Owned by Camille Kam, Kido was trained for Obedience at 10 years of age by Bill Bobrow and proceeded to acquire his degree at this ripe age. He may well be the oldest Akita to earn a CD.

mention. For those who wish to get started, we have included a summary of AKC Companion Dog (CD) competition below. Advanced competition for Companion Dog Excellent (CDX) and Utility Dog (UD) titles will require teaching your dog to work at a distance, retrieve, jump and do scent work. We hope you enjoy the experience.

Notes on the Author

Bill Bobrow has had Akitas since 1982. His dogs have won many high-scoring Akita awards at Specialties, two awards of Merit at the 1992 Akita National Specialty, number one Obedience Akita

SUNDOWNER'S MIKO'S ROKKI SAN, owned and trained by Cathy M. Dunn, shown performing the various Agility exercises.

Agility Dog Walk.
Courtesy V. Hartronft.

Agility See Saw.
Courtesy V. Hartronft.

Agility Window.
Courtesy V. Hartronft.

124

Agility Hoop Jump.
Courtesy V. Hartronft.

Agility A-Frame.
Courtesy V. Hartronft.

Agility Spread Jump.
Courtesy V. Hartronft.

in 1988 and numbers one, two and three Top Obedience Akitas of 1990. His dogs have placed in the Top Ten Obedience Akitas in eight different years. Bill owns and trained the most titled Akita bitch in the history of the breed. A writer of training articles, Bill also works with rescue Akitas for the Akita Rescue Society of America. He is the ACA Public Education Chairman on the breed and training director for Mojave Greens K-9 Training Club. In addition, the achievements of dogs Bill has owned or trained include many AKC championships, CD and CDX titles and Mexican and International championships, PC titles and International Best in Show awards.

Two Firsts—Ch. Sukoshi Kuma, CDX

Sukoshi holds two records of firsts in the breed. Owned by Dr. Gilbert Roth, Sukoshi was the first Akita to earn an AKC championship and the first Akita champion to earn a CDX.

Dr. Roth, who is an approved AKC Obedience judge, says, "We were proud of Sukoshi's accomplishments. They were important to us. I would have to say, though, that his place in our family was most important. Sukoshi brought us the kind of joy and companionship that made him first in the hearts of those whose lives he touched."

POWER PULLING

Undefeated in the sport in 1978, Ch. Remwood Sashi Motto was owned and trained by Bill and Sharon Howard. As Bill said, "For those who have some spare time and a healthy dog, this sport is as contagious as the show ring. It also keeps your dog in fantastic condition and gives dogs that added attention so often missed during the winter months."

According to his owner, Sashi pulled a roller tamper over a new lawn, and pulled Christmas trees off mountains as well as other feats. Unofficially, he has pulled 2,300 pounds and 1,700 pounds in competition. Sashi lived in Montana and he was a remarkable Akita.

CH. NAMI'S SHOKKO OF OKA, CD, owned by Cindy and Ned Ratterman. This Akita was the #1 Obedience Akita 1991 (Novice) Akita World System II and also was in top ten Obedience Akitas in 1989 and 1990.

Author's note: The Cascade Akita Club had early involvement with power pulling and Akitas. Contact the ACA (Parent Club) for address.

DOG SLEDDING

David and Karen Elson started with Malamutes and ended up with Akitas involved in the sport of dog sledding.

David said his dogs averaged speeds of fifteen to twenty miles per hour for twenty-plus mile distances. In his words, "Both the dogs and owner benefit physically and mentally from the rigors of the sport. The key elements necessary are attitude and *soundness* on the part of the dogs, and patience on the owner's part. All involved will reap the benefits and enjoyment of the sport."

127

AM/CAN CH. CHARISMA'S MIKO-GO NO K MIKADO, UDT, SchH III. The owner/ trainer/handler is Janice Mitchell.

SCHUTZHUND

One of the most qualified persons to comment on this dramatic sport may well be Janice Mitchell of Washington State. Her Akita is Am. & Can. Ch. Charisma's Miko Go No K Mikado, UDT, SchH III.

Janice and her husband, Steve, feel that training should start at eight weeks, or when you finally acquire your puppy if later than that. Leash work, household manners, building a rapport with your dog and bonding are all imperative in the beginning. It is felt that the average Akita is quite independent and will take advantage of a lax trainer. "Trust is of primary importance," according to the Mitchells.

Miko and Janice worked at fairs, searched for lost children

CH. TRIPLE K SHOYU-GO, CD. Shown to all titles by his owner, Lurean (Micki) Guthrie of Reno, Nevada, Shoyu was equally at home as a Schutzhund-trained Akita. Micki used the Hashi prefix for her breeding.

and helped the police in making arrests and quelling riots. Miko will always hold a special place in the Mitchells' hearts and thoughts.

THE AKITA AS A HUNTER

Larry Shepherd and his Akita male, Shiro-E-Ashi-San (Mr. Whitefeet), were in the field together from the time Shiro was four months old until he was nine years of age. As the result of an unfortunate accident, Shiro was finally retired to the post of camp guardian. Larry's story will always be timely for those who would consider hunting as a sport with their Akita.

Protection and Schutzhund work. Don and Carol Thorne's SHORU-GO was a brindle import who served the Kern County, California Sheriff's Department. Working in the K-9 unit, Shoru was an example of what a properly trained Akita can do, serving in the department with seven German Shepherds. He finally retired and lived to nine years of age. He was indeed a remarkable dual-purpose dog.

Trying to unravel the tremendous potential of the Akita is like pulling teeth with eyebrow tweezers. The capabilities are there, but those interested in finding out what this breed can do are few and far between. Most owners accept the fact that the Akita is an excellent home companion or show dog and that is as far as it goes.

Ancient writings from their native land, Japan, tell us that some Akitas were originally used not only as fighting dogs but also to hunt bear. Though this in itself should tend to raise the eyebrows of big-game hunters, very few owners in this country have taken their dogs into the field and conscientiously worked with them to determine their hunting capabilities. We

130

have only scratched the surface in determining the full hunting potential of this breed, though we have verified that the Akita has a hunting background. Any experienced hunter can observe an Akita in the field for ten minutes and conclude that the ancestral lineage was wild and woolly. This conclusion is confirmed by writings telling of Akita ancestors being scarred by the tusks of wild boar and of their fights with the native Japanese Yezo Bear.

The Akita has the mental and physical characteristics necessary to be an excellent hunter, combining natural hunting instincts with intelligence. The breed readily adapts to gunfire and I have heard of few Akitas that are gun-shy. Scenting ability compares favorably with many of our sporting breeds and the Akita's hearing is better than average. They are silent hunters and will often adopt a sneak approach when closing in on game they have scented. Though fearless, Akitas advance with caution on game they have sighted and they appear to

CH. OKII YUBI'S SNOW JO, CDX, TD.

131

LANGAN'S MAKKURO BUSHI-GO, TDX.

size up a target before attacking. Akitas as a breed are tough and strong with a surprising lateral quickness that keeps them out of trouble when confronted by large and dangerous game.

The Akita has been used with a measure of success as a flusher and is an exceptionally good retriever on land. Though many publicity articles have stated that they are powerful swimmers, I have found them to be poor swimmers in comparison with our well-known water retrievers. Large bone structure and a water-absorbing coat is not conducive to buoyancy in water. Even so, Akitas will retrieve ducks brought down close to shore.

They are not trackers in the hound sense, but have been known to follow a blood trail to conclusion. Because of a natural ability and love for hunting, the Akita will do a respectable job on any type of small or medium game. However, once introduced to big game, the adult is separated from the pup.

Having hunted with many so-called deer dogs, I can state without equivocation that none of those I have seen can compare with the Akita on this type of game. On several occasions, my dog has scented and pointed herds of deer between 200 and 300 yards away. On one specific occasion, he alerted and followed the scent for a measured 125 yards, where he jumped a small, bedded-down deer. On one late afternoon and evening hunt, he scented, sighted or jumped nine deer I never would have seen on my own. He is at his best when checking out thickly wooded and brush-covered patches. Working down-wind, he will immediately alert if there are deer in these areas.

It is my opinion the Akita will turn out to be a surprise package for those taking the time and trouble to do the un-wrapping!

Dr. Jeffrey P. Fowler with his Akita guide dog, MOTO-YURI'S COVER GIRL DOTTIE.

9

"Dottie"—The Story of an Akita Guide Dog

by Bill Bobrow

FOR TWO MONTHS I had waited for a final decision on how our experiment had worked. Now I had it in writing. An Akita sent to me by Andi Maloon was soon to become a guide dog for a practicing cardiologist named Jeff Fowler. I read the letter over and over, wanting to make sure I had not misread anything, at the same time enjoying the feeling of success with each reading. Each time I finished the letter, my thoughts shifted to the life Jeff and Dottie would soon be spending together. I hoped this was the beginning of many fruitful years for Jeff and his new partner. I also thought about the many wonderful relationships I had developed because of Dottie, and I remembered our first encounter.

May 27, 1992

Dr. Jeffrey P. Fowler
3450 Woodside Road
Louisville, KY 40222

Dear Dr. Fowler:

Our Trainers have worked with and observed Dottie and we are
pleased to tell you that she is coming along in good fashion. She
has perked up and we have noticed a fine response, especially
with the cooler weather.

Our Trainer that has spent the most time with her feels she should
be ready by June 21st and we realize this might be too fast for
your plans and, therefore, it would be perfectly alright to schedule
you for July 12th. Either date will fit into our plans and now it is
just to hear from you and what is best for your schedule.

Indeed, we are happy to make this report and will wait until we
hear from you.

Sincerely yours,

John J. Gray
Executive Director

*(She's very obedient and we are now working on a little stronger
pull—at this point all looks good! John)*

Here she was, coming off an airplane, having flown all the
way from Louisville, Kentucky. She should have been scared or at
least reticent. She wasn't. Andi had described Dottie as nonaggres-
sive. My fear was that this also meant somewhat shy. Andi had
said no to my concern and was right. This girl was confident. She
was also starting to awkwardly stretch into growth. I wished I had
gotten her sooner. She was almost five months old now and I had
wanted to start her when I often start my own puppies, by ten or
twelve weeks.

Blessed by her ignorance, she didn't know what we faced. She was curious, friendly and gentle. She immediately seemed like a good dog to train. Our goal was to make her into Jeff's companion and guide dog.

Andi had originally called me in May 1991 and asked if I would like to raise and do preliminary training on a guide dog Akita for Dr. Jeff Fowler. She explained he would need the dog within two years. The diagnosis Dr. Fowler had received about his eyesight was that it was deteriorating and he would soon not be able to get around without a great deal of assistance. In truth, Dr. Fowler was already legally blind.

Jeff Fowler is a young-looking fellow who has practiced medicine for over twenty years, and he wasn't ready to retire. He wanted to give a guide dog a try, but he didn't want just any dog. He wanted an Akita.

AN AKITA AS A GUIDE DOG?

When Andi and I first spoke about Dottie, I was flattered at being asked to do something so important, but was wary of getting overly excited. It was my understanding that over half of the dogs that begin guide dog training never make it through. I wasn't even sure how my training methods would apply. A guide dog has to pull and be aware of everything going on around it. An Obedience dog was not supposed to pull and only needs to be aware of its master. Would my training help or hurt a prospective guide dog?

I began talking to different trainers and calling around to guide dog facilities. People there were pleasant and helpful. They seemed to convey that if a dog had what it took, the dog could be trained to do the job.

Pretraining was important but most important was that the dog be confident and a good learner. Each potential guide dog needed exposure to every imaginable everyday situation; all training was a plus. The dog had to be willing to assume responsibility and lead. I was warned that quite often Obedience dogs would not pull. Nevertheless, the literature I received had basic instructions on how to

Obedience-train a dog. The literature encouraged training; the methods recommended were practically the same as those I normally use.

PILOT DOGS

The guide dog institutions I contacted in California were not interested in working with an Akita, but one lady with whom I spoke referred me to Pilot Dogs in Columbus, Ohio. I conveyed the information to Andi Maloon and she spoke to the people at Pilot Dogs. They were willing to consider her idea.

The trainers at Pilot Dogs had worked with a variety of breeds and were willing to give it a shot if they found Dottie acceptable for their program. They weren't really sure what an Akita looked like, and they understood that Akitas were too large and aggressive to do guide dog work. When I talked to them they warned me that fewer than half the dogs they start with actually make it through their program. However, they were curious and willing to try.

John Gray, the Executive Director of Pilot Dogs, let me know that our Akita had to have a good temperament and good health. They would take a look at her at one to one-and-a-half years of age and decide to accept her or not.

I felt we had a chance but I wasn't overly confident. I was being given one specific dog and asked to prepare it for one specific person. The odds did not sound great. I decided the worst that could happen would be failure. But, after all, Dr. Fowler could still find himself a guide dog, albeit not an Akita.

Pilot Dogs did not want to invest their time and money into a dog with little chance of making it through the program. If Dottie had hip or other health problems, it would not work. If she spooked easily, it also would not work. And if she were too big, it would not work. If her stride did not match Dr. Fowler's, it would not work. If she were stubborn, not trainable or unable to assume the responsibility of leading, it would not work. Many potential problems stood between us and our goal.

WILL SHE QUALIFY?

I was especially concerned about Dottie's health. I've trained a number of Akitas only to find out they suffer from hip dysplasia, loose patellas (knees), cruciate ligament problems or autoimmune diseases. Was I going to invest up to one year raising and working with Dottie only to find that she couldn't function as a working dog because of health problems? I knew that Andi and co-breeder Tamara Warren were concerned about these problems and were trying to breed for health. But breeders, sometimes breeding for show winning and not working ability, had left a genetic legacy on the breed. I had been stung more than once with beautiful, trainable puppies who lacked soundness and health as adults.

I was less concerned about Dottie's temperament. There is no doubt that some Akitas are spooky, overly aggressive or difficult to train, but these are in the minority. The breed as a whole is calm, intelligent, trainable and loyal. The majority of Akitas can be dog-aggressive toward the same sex, but in most cases this can be controlled with socialization, good training and care in handling. If Dottie showed some aggression later, I would have to face it and attempt to control it enough to be safe for a blind man. Although every Akita temperament is certainly not fit for guide work, I've trained a few Akitas with guide potential. I knew that the myth of Akitas not being trainable is nonsense.

I was anxious about my task. First, I wasn't positive I knew what the guide dog trainers were looking for, and second, I could only make an educated guess about our puppy's soundness and ultimate size. I'm told that Dottie has now outgrown her 24-inch size limit, imposed so that she could fit into small spaces. Fortunately, she has turned out sound and healthy.

These were the problems we saw. Now it was time to start work. Dottie was here now and she seemed temperamentally suited. As a backup, I obtained another female puppy whose parents I knew. If I could have, I would have used four pups to start with. I wanted to raise my odds of success as much as possible.

DOTTIE'S TRAINING

I began training Dottie and her backup, Molly, almost immediately. I knew how important it would be for a guide dog to get along with other dogs and animals, so my house became home for the two girls and a young female Shiba named Otsu. I also had two cats that spent most of their time in the house putting up with the young dogs.

Dottie and Molly did fine. They got along with Otsu and the cats, they were quick learners and they were outgoing. I began taking them to parks and matches and working them in different environments, including traffic-filled downtown Los Angeles, crowded elevators and escalators. Dottie was the more adaptable of the two.

After I'd had the girls about six weeks, I took them to a match just so they could mix and I could see how they reacted to the park environment. They played with the kids who took them for walks and tried to play with the many pups and dogs who were there to show. Toward the end of the day, I ran a little test on my guide puppies. I had both Dottie and Molly lying down in front of a loudspeaker being used by the announcer of the match. Lacking a pole, the speaker had been placed on a chair. The dogs were placed in front of the chair during a lull in the announcing. The volume on the speaker was annoyingly loud; I was interested in the dogs' reactions. When the announcer came back on the speaker, Dottie calmly held her position, but Molly bolted. Neither pup was yet seven months old, but Dottie's special temperament was apparent.

Further into our training, we took a ride on an escalator. It took Molly two trips to gain confidence while Dottie adjusted after a few seconds. Metal grating in the sidewalks bothered Molly, but not Dottie. It became obvious that Dottie was the better dog to send to Jeff. Perhaps Molly could be effectively trained, but Dottie was a natural. Traffic, trucks, tractors, crowds, buildings were all taken in stride by Dottie. She was indeed a special dog. Through friends, I found a home for Molly and devoted myself completely to Dottie.

We did not train every day or for long periods of time. Mostly we spent time together, learning our manners doing some traveling and meeting people. Dottie usually lived in the house, but for a few

140

"DOTTIE" and Bill Bobrow's granddaughter, Chelsey, when Dottie was a puppy in training.

weeks at a time I would put her in a dog run and some evenings in a dog crate. I tried to move her around so she would be used to different situations. For a week at a time she might see me only at feeding time. The rest of the time she would be in a dog run surrounded by other dogs. At other times, she would spend the time playing with my three-year-old granddaughter, Chelsey.

Dottie was a joy to have around. Gentle, responsive, intelligent, she was also protective and acted like a guard dog with strangers or animals outside our yard. Her protective instincts were always evident. At one point, she began placing herself between me, other people and animals. When the other dogs came looking for pats or behind-the-ear scratches, Dottie would lean against me and circle, keeping the other dogs from touching me. She and the other dogs never growled. They were simply pushed away. It seemed to me that she would have to be more open to approaches from people and animals; I worked to break this habit.

I decided she was too attached to me. She would soon have to adapt to the Pilot Dog trainers, then to Jeff. I contacted Lille Hoye, a trainer with whom I've worked since I began training. She agreed to work with Dottie for a few weeks. They did basic Obedience work and the result was excellent. When Dottie came back, her protective instinct was better controlled and she had gained some maturity which reflected in more precise work.

Dottie's Obedience training was not unusual. She began Sits, Downs, Stands, Heeling and Recalls as any dog learning Obedience would do. Pilot Dogs recommended that guide dogs be trained without bait, and I quickly found that Dottie was more interested in pleasing me than she was in food. Her training rewards consisted almost exclusively of praise, which she accepted graciously with a happy look and wag of the tail.

Our training sessions were as short as a few minutes every other day but gradually became longer. We trained in different areas and often worked in my bird yard among the chickens, geese, ducks and pigeons.

Dottie's attention span and stamina were stretched by trips to different Obedience classes. We dropped in at classes at Red Arrow kennel where we practiced our basics with Eleanor Heist and Lille Hoye. We also practiced with these ladies many evenings as we sharpened our skills with their guidance. Dottie and I enrolled in Bill Fischer's Hi-Desert Obedience Club class. The other classes we attended were held by Carleen Newman. She and her assistants, Carol and Tanya, really helped in proofing Dottie. It was not unusual to find large pieces of chicken, biscuits or bones lying around in the middle of our heeling area. Dottie often found herself in a Down-Stay next to a meaty beef bone. The classes also featured blank pistols, banging trash cans and flying plastic bags.

People were really curious and helpful when they learned that Dottie was working to become a guide dog. A few people were skeptical at first, but after I had her a few weeks and especially after meeting Dottie, the real animal lovers became Dottie's cheer-leaders. As Dottie completed training, it was fun to see others get excited about the prospect of a guide dog Akita. People didn't mind our coming into their homes for practice and were always amazed by Dottie's gentle nature and good manners.

A week or two before we left, Dottie was allowed to attend a party with most of the active members of the Inland Empire Akita Club. She mingled easily with the many people and kids at the party, took no food off the coffee tables and soon joined in the kids' chase and hide games. As one person noted, "She's just like one of the kids." At this point I was very proud of her and becoming confident that she would make it at Pilot Dogs.

Our first moment of truth was approaching. Andi and Jeff had made arrangements for Dottie and me to fly to Louisville where Dottie was to compete in an Obedience trial before going up to Columbus to meet the people at Pilot Dogs. We spent a few days with Sandy and Jeff Fowler. Dottie seemed to remember them and their place. She took to Jeff immediately, and seemed to know they had a special relationship. During her stay at my home, Jeff had sent Dottie his heavily scented T-shirt and his voice on tape. I'll never know if these things helped her remember him, but the interaction was obvious. Dottie slept in Jeff and Sandy's room and was a hit wherever she went.

On Sunday, March 15, 1992, Dottie was Highest Scoring Dog at the Akita Club of America Regional Specialty held in conjunction with the Louisville Kennel Club show. Dottie's first birthday would be March 23.

THE EVALUATION

On Monday morning, March 16, the Fowlers, Andi Maloon, Dottie and I left for Columbus, Ohio. We had an appointment to meet with John Gray at Pilot Dogs to see if Dottie would be accepted into their program.

Dottie was about to be heavily scrutinized. I had brought hip X-rays and blood tests as I had been asked. Dottie had seemed a bit overwhelmed at times since arriving in Louisville. She was, after all, less than a year old, confronted with dog shows, new environment, new people, full days and constant attention. I'm sure she was also aware of the anxiety of the other passengers in Andi's car as we traveled to Ohio.

At Pilot Dogs, we all sat down to talk with Mr. Gray in the lobby of the facility. Pilot Dogs has been around a number of years and is a respected organization. At that time, they had about fifty dogs being raised in homes. Their own facilities house about 120 dogs in training. We saw many trainers and a number of blind people and dogs going through their one month in-residence training program. If Dottie was accepted and completed the four-month training program satisfactorily, Jeff would soon become a resident student.

Dottie's evaluation began almost immediately. Her health tests were fine. As we sat in the lobby chatting, she was being observed. She forgot all about me and seemed intent on being around Jeff. She was exposed to two life-size models of dogs in the lobby, showed curiosity and cautiously barked at one of them.

Curiosity among the office workers and trainers was obvious. Wayne, the head trainer, took her for a walk while the rest of us talked. We had some time later to talk, and we exchanged some thoughts about training, evaluating puppies, temperaments and Akitas. He said books presented Akitas as too aggressive for guide dog work. The first thing he had done when he took Dottie for his walk was to approach other dogs at the facility. No aggression was displayed. Wayne was obviously very cautious about making a commitment to train Dottie.

He took her for a walk around the block and noted that she was nervous and had defecated along the way. I was surprised and suggested that I walk Dottie while he observed. This time she did much better. She ignored the cars, trucks, trash pickup, open shop doors, chicken bones on the sidewalk and rattling fences. She was nervous when Wayne walked about eighteen inches behind her for a stretch but settled as we continued walking. This time she performed well. When we came back, Dottie ignored me and settled at Jeff's feet.

Next, Wayne suggested that Jeff go for a walk with him and a Doberman Pinscher that was in training for guide dog work. Andi, Sandy and I walked quietly behind at a distance. Jeff was led by the dog as Wayne walked along by his side. It was interesting to see the Doberman work. She did well at ignoring the commotion and stopping at curbs, but moved toward the chicken bones and wanted to visit the people inside an open shop building. Dottie hadn't done too badly after all. I felt that the Doberman must have walked these streets many times and that our Akita was a steadier dog. When we all returned, John Gray asked his trainer if he could work with Dottie. The answer was yes.

The tension left us but I knew this was only another new beginning. Dottie still had to complete her guide dog course. Jeff and Andi seemed to be the most confident, with Jeff telling us later that he wasn't happy with the Doberman and that Dottie would do just fine at the school. We were all elated.

A NEW BEGINNING

Andi completed some paperwork and Dottie was left to begin a new chapter in her life. I hadn't expected it to happen so suddenly. Dottie was now a schoolgirl living at the dorms and we were on our way back to Kentucky. That was the last time I saw Dottie. I know I'll see her again. I've talked to her owner over the phone, but I'll still miss her.

This was not the end of the story. I kept in contact with the Maloons, the Fowlers and Pilot Dogs as Dottie prepared for her new life. It was not all smooth sailing. At first Pilot Dogs raved about how obedient Dottie was and how fast she was progressing. Then they became concerned about her being nervous and pushy around other dogs.

Jeff and Andi asked me to talk to the people at Pilot Dogs about her problems. After some discussion with John Gray, I surmised that Dottie was an instant curiosity among the trainers. They all wanted to work with her and it appears they all took turns with her. After discussions with Andi, I told John that Dottie was too young for so much change in lifestyle and people all at one time. I suggested she had a need to bond and be worked by just one trainer or that I would take her back for a few months while she matured.

John Gray spoke knowledgeably to me about Dottie and indicated that Wayne would be in charge of her training and adjustments would be made. The rest of Dottie's progress reports were excellent. She completed her training in about two-and-a-half months, ahead of schedule.

Jeff joined Dottie at Pilot Dogs for their team training. He told me that their final test would be a snap, and it was. Jeff was more worried about himself passing than about Dottie doing her job. Both passed the test in which they had to do some everyday things like shop and take a bus on their own.

Today, Jeff and Dottie can be seen happily roaming hospital corridors and rooms as Jeff visits his patients. They have become quite a team. The biggest problem Dottie has is that everyone wants to pet her. The biggest problem Jeff has is that he doesn't know if his patients are more happy to see him or Dottie.

He thinks it is Dottie.

EPILOGUE
by Virginia Funk

Reprinted by permission from *Dog Lover's Digest*.

THIS MOMENT IS MAGIC

Come, share the magic of this moment.
He walks through the still leaves of darkness
The light and shade falling through trees about him.
Drifts of daffodils glow like candles on the earth;
Seedlings are a sparkle of emerald stars.
At rest his guide dog nestles like a jewel
   at his feet.
Honesty is substituted for speed;
Courage for desperation and
Stamina for self-consciousness.
He has overcome a handicap
To give a thrilling performance
And has, at least, added a touch of greatness
   to his life.

10

Breeding and Whelping

$\mathbf{Y}$OU'VE REALLY PREPARED for this day. You've chosen an excellent stud well ahead of time and you're hopeful that the bitch and the dog will complement each other. If you're linebreeding, you've made sure they have high-quality common ancestors in the first three generations. The breeding contracts have been read, understood and signed by both parties.

You have kept your bitch in prime physical condition. Your veterinarian has checked her, she has had a laboratory fecal exam to check for internal parasites and her immunizations including parvovirus have been brought up to date. A vaccination booster near the time of breeding will give pups greater immunity against the common puppy diseases. She's had an X-ray to determine she is free of hip dysplasia and a blood test to be sure she doesn't have brucellosis. You have also asked for and received proof from the stud dog's owner that the dog is free of hip dysplasia and has had a brucellosis test and that his immunizations are up to date.

You took all these precautions because you want your puppies to be healthy and adhere closely to the Standard of perfection as set down by the Akita Club of America through the American Kennel Club. All in all, you feel like a parent who has arranged a marriage.

READY—OR NOT?

Your bitch may be ready for breeding as early as the seventh or eighth day or as late as the twenty-third day of her estrus (heat cycle). The average is between the tenth and fourteenth days. Some bitches are able to conceive for just a few hours; others have a span of several days. Consecutive vaginal smears taken by your veterinarian several days apart can be used as a guide.

If your bitch is to be shipped to her mate, it is important to send her far enough into her heat period so the trip won't stop the season, *but* soon enough to give her time to rest and become acclimated to her surroundings before she is bred. If she is accompanied by someone she knows, she will be even more relaxed. But if she must travel alone, insist that the stud's owner or agent have two witnesses verify in writing that a breeding was consummated between your bitch and the stud you selected as per the breeding contract.

If you have chosen a local stud, it is wise, on arrival at his kennel, for you and the dog's owner to introduce the two dogs *on lead* or put them in adjacent pens. A maiden bitch may be frightened if immediately put with a strange stud. There is also a chance she could be an unwilling breeder, in which case there could be quite a row. It is always wise to safeguard against dogs or bitches being injured.

If the two Akitas seem fairly affable, release them in a confined area for courtship. Allow plenty of time, especially if the bitch is new to all of this. When she is ready, she will stand for the male and flag her tail to one side. Play it by ear. If she sits down with a puzzled look on her face when her suitor advances, they will both need more than moral support. A gentle assist under the bitch's hindquarters may be all that is required.

Some bitches refuse to be bred even though they are physiologically ready. Although force breeding is not pleasant, it can be

The pups whelped by Ch. Sanmark Sunfire of Northland have left the whelping box and are ready to explore their surroundings.

accomplished. It may indeed be the only way to get a recalcitrant bitch bred. Simply muzzle her and hold her still. You might find that the ''I'd rather do it myself'' stud dogs don't always perform under these circumstances.

Mother Nature has a nice process of selective breeding. If not physically or psychologically reproducible, the undesirable trait is not perpetuated in future generations. Let's face it. Not all ''physically perfect'' bitches should be bred.

THE BREEDING

If the mating is successful, a ''tie'' is accomplished between the two. During the tie, the stud dismounts, turns, and the two stand on all fours, posterior to posterior until the tie is over. It is interesting to note the end-to-end position dogs assume during mating is an evolutionary selection process. Because of the length of the tie, and being end to end, the so engaged animals were better able to defend themselves from predators. An inexperienced male may need assistance to reach this position.

While the two Akitas are tied, both stud and bitch owners should hold their dogs' heads, comfort them if necessary and restrain

149

them from attempting to break away. It is not unusual for the bitch to yelp and whine all through the tie as if she were in total agony. Do not despair. No real harm is being done. When the tie ends naturally (anywhere from five to forty-five minutes), separate them and offer them a cool drink of water. You may repeat the breeding every other day until she no longer accepts him. This is an especially good idea if it is the stud's first breeding assignment.

From one to three weeks after being bred, a bitch may develop a vaginal infection if dirt was introduced during breeding. Watch for a discharge and make a quick visit to the vet if you see one.

THE PREGNANCY

About five weeks after breeding, the bitch may appear a little rounded through her hips and abdomen. You may want your vet to verify her pregnancy. The bitch's appetite may increase by the fifth week. This is the time to add to her food intake. The meals should have the correct amount of protein and calcium per body weight. Because of space taken up by the growing pups, meals broken into twice-a-day feedings are recommended. Remember, as a general rule *a fat bitch does not whelp easily*, so don't stuff your Akita indiscriminately. It has been suggested to withhold vitamin and mineral supplements (especially calcium) until the last trimester. Exercise your Akita regularly, in moderation, to keep her trim.

Water must always be available. It helps prevent constipation and maintain good health. *Do not try any home remedies. Many such medicines designed for humans can be lethal for dogs.* And be on guard against well-meaning friends who have a cure for anything that may go wrong with your bitch. Listen politely, thank them for their advice, then call your veterinarian to learn what to do.

Exercise is important to maintain muscle tone and to aid in a speedy and easy whelping. Violent exercise and jumping are to be avoided. As the bitch becomes heavier she will most likely limit her actions. Many bitches who used to be the first one in on a family wrestle now will sit sedately on the sidelines.

Everyday grooming is a good idea. Not only will it keep the

150

mother-to-be's skin in good condition and her coat clean, she will have that little bit of extra attention so vital while she is in "the family way." Should some unforeseen skin infection or other ailment arise, you will discover it quickly in a daily grooming session.

Toward the end of the pregnancy, keep your bitch's belly clean by bathing it with bland soap. The hair surrounding the nipples will gradually begin to fall out, preparing her body for the coming event.

SUPPLIES

The Whelping Box

The most important piece of equipment to have in readiness for the big event is the whelping box. Made of plywood, it should be large enough for the bitch to stretch out in all directions when she is nursing, with room left over for the pups to move around in as they mature. One-and-a-half times the length of the bitch is a good rule of thumb. If it is too big, puppies can wander away from the warmth of the nest and unduly exasperate the new mother.

The sides should be high enough to keep the pups in, but low enough to let Mom out easily. Four inches up from the flooring, a 1-inch-by-4-inch smooth wooden board should be attached to the sides, with small angle irons all around as a rail. This will prevent the bitch from accidentally smothering to death any puppy that crawls behind her. You might also consider raising your box a few inches off the floor, especially if it's on a concrete floor or you live in a cold climate. If your box is not raised, do put a layer of heavy construction-type plastic under it to prevent dampness.

After you have made your box, layer its floor with a generous padding of newspaper. It is easier to peel off soiled sheets of paper during and after whelping than it is to move mother and babies from one corner to the next while you lay new paper.

As the whelping box is being constructed, your bitch will show no interest. She may go about digging holes in the yard, her own way of preparing her nest. The box should, for this reason, be constructed and put in place at least two weeks in advance of whelping so that she can be encouraged to sleep in it. If she has a favorite rug or toy, place it in the pen to help her understand that she is to nest there instead of under the house!

The Outside Pen

Another, but not immediate, need is an outside pen. This should be mobile. A discarded baby playpen is often useful for this purpose. Sunshine and fresh air promote healthy pups; the outside pen can be put into use when the pups are about three weeks old.

Some precautions should be noted:

- If you are going to use an old-fashioned playpen with wood slats, cover the entire outside with small-holed wire mesh, making sure the nails or brads attaching it to the slats do not protrude inside. Not only will this type of covering prevent the pups from escaping when they are tiny, they will be unable to get stuck between the rails when they are bigger.
- The pen must be situated so the pups have both sunshine and shade at all times and not be in drafty areas.
- **The pups should never be left alone in the pen when you are away from the house**, even for a few minutes. There are too many interested people with poor intentions in this world.

The First-Aid Kit

Last but not least is the first-aid kit. Some items mentioned here may not be used by everyone, but it is wise to have most of these on hand:

1. Box lined with towels for the pups
2. Heating pad or hot water bottle to keep pup box warm
3. Pile of clean terry-cloth towels to dry the pups
4. Stack of newspapers (You will need every paper you can lay your hands on. Ask everyone you know to save theirs for you. Don't wait until the last minute. It is unbelievable how fast they will be used up.)
5. K-Y jelly, *un*opened tube

Akitas appreciate a comfortable home. Pictured is Ch. NAN CHAO'S FOX OF HIDDEN ACRE.

6. Rubber gloves
7. Soap
8. Betadine or Tincture of Iodine to sterilize ends of umbilical cords
9. Blunt scissors to cut umbilical cords
10. Betadine to keep scissors sterilized
11. Lightweight monofilament fishing line to tie off umbilical cords
12. Rectal thermometer
13. Flashlight
14. Waste container
15. Baby scale to weigh each pup at birth
16. Clock
17. Sleeping bag or cot (for you)
18. Pencil and paper to record whelping details. The memory alone is not a reliable source. Write everything down: any

unusual detail of labor, the length of the labor, the birth time of each pup and each pup's description including weight at birth.

19. Soft tissues to use in absorbing mucus from nose and mouth

THE WHELPING

Puppies are normally born between the fifty-eighth and sixty-fifth day after breeding, the sixty-third day being average. One sign of impending motherhood is when the bitch's temperature falls from the average 100.5–101.5 degrees F. to about 99–100 degrees F. A dip in temperature for any length of time could mean whelping is about to begin. It may be a matter of hours or a couple of days, but it is an encouraging sign.

How do you take a dog's temperature? Have the bitch stand up or lie down on one side. Lubricate the rectal thermometer with Vaseline and insert into the rectum 1½ inches or so. Hold your fingers close to the thermometer just in case the bitch moves suddenly. Talk to her and soothe her. *Important:* Never leave her for a moment while the thermometer is inserted. Let that phone ring. If a family crisis occurs, start again later but *never leave her!*

Two minutes after insertion is ample time for an accurate reading, but we do suggest you take the temperature a couple of times a day and at the same time every day, preferably not after eating or exercising.

Restlessness is another sign that whelping will soon begin. Pamper your bitch and remain calm. You are her steadying force. She will dig holes and pace. She is reacting to her most basic instincts. Encourage her to use the whelping box.

Speaking of basic instincts, *the whelping area will be more acceptable to your bitch if it is removed from the mainstream of family traffic* and, if possible, dimly lighted. Wild dogs prefer caves and holes. Although you may not like to think of your sweet Mesu (the Japanese term for female dog) as basically wild, a deep-seated instinct to nest as her ancestors did is still very much there. So help her to satisfy her needs where you can.

154

When one or both of the aforementioned signs of whelping shows, turn your attention to the whelping area itself. Temperature should be between 80 and 85 degrees F. for the first two weeks of the pups' lives. Be alert for drafts and dampness. An *electric heater* may be used *near* the pen, *never* directly *over* it. Put a *thermometer* at floor level of the pen, *not in it*, so there will be no question of temperature. Some breeders use a *heat lamp* over the pen. We suggest you discuss this with your veterinarian.

Where and when the bitch first strains and has her first pup can be anyone's guess. Rarely will she pick a time when it is light out and the dishes are washed! It will probably be soon after you have settled in for the night. So grab your robe and slippers and be ready to aid her.

Lists and precautions whiz through your head. In the long run Mother Nature and common sense win out most of the time. Your flighty little female suddenly becomes the most matronly of mothers, tossing away those carefree days of irresponsibility and settling into her nest to whelp her young. Hopefully she has picked her whelping box and not a mud puddle in the middle of a thunderstorm!

Speaking of mud puddles, a word to the wise. If you are taking your bitch out to relieve herself either just before whelping or during whelping, take along another person, a pair of scissors, a towel and, if it is nighttime, a flashlight. She may decide your flower bed is a romantic place to relieve herself . . . of a puppy. If she does, you are prepared.

Whelping time is most unpredictable and depends on litter size, age and experience of the bitch, mothering instincts, etc. During the **first stage of labor**, the passages are stretching and softening. Very often the bitch will pace. She may even yelp or whimper once in a while. She may rip apart every paper in her carefully prepared whelping box and wash herself so frequently you are sure the skin will wear off.

During the **second stage of labor**, she is content to lie down and is happy to have you with her. Warning: Do not ask your neighbors to come and watch. You do not want the bitch to become apprehensive. Only members of the immediate family should be allowed to stay, provided they remain quiet and calm. Use your own discretion about children. The mother will probably be breathing deeply now and will clench her paws as contractions begin. She will be panting in between.

As the contractions become stronger, the panting becomes steady. The eyes may become slightly glazed. Then, miracle of miracles, a watery fluid seeps from the vulva, sometimes with a soft popping noise. The tail arches and with one or more contractions, a pup arrives. An especially large pup may cause the bitch to strain a bit more before delivery.

Puppies can be born headfirst or hind feet first (breech). Both positions are normal.

Most Akita bitches are quite capable of taking care of every detail of the whelping. Some are even awed by it all. These consider themselves fascinated observers as the first couple of pups present themselves. You can help here and later on if your new mother should tire.

Each pup is born in a membraneous sac of water. An umbilical cord leads from the sac to the placenta. If the bitch fails to clean the membrane off the pup's head immediately, you must so the pup can start breathing. You may insert your finger in the pup's mouth with absorbent tissue to clear the breathing passages if it is necessary.

If the bitch does not cut the cord, let the newborn lie for a moment while the blood in the cord flows into the pup, then tie the cord in two places with the lightest weight monofilament fishing line. Using sterile scissors, cut between the two ties, about two inches from the pup's abdomen, and daub the end with Betadine or Tincture of Iodine.

As each membrane is removed and the cry of life is given, your heart skips a beat and perhaps a tear of emotion runs down your cheek. But while it is a time for reverence, it is also a time for action. Keep two things in mind: Newborn pups need *warmth* and *fluids*. If the mother does not start licking the pup to dry and stimulate it, your handy stack of towels comes into action. Check the mouth and nostrils to make sure they are clear. Rub the pup until it is dry and warm.

After each pup comes the spongy **placenta** or afterbirth, which your bitch may consume even before she cares for the pup. Don't worry. This is a natural instinct. In the wild, the afterbirths served as the bitch's only source of food for several days while she looked after her newly whelped litter.

It is imperative that you check for each afterbirth, because it is vital they all be expelled. If they are not, the bitch could get a uterine infection that can endanger her life and her litter. These suggestions are not made to scare you. They are given for your peace of mind so that you can enjoy this whole, marvelous experience free of worry.

Each pup is born with a waxy plug, **meconium**, about one-inch long, in the large intestine. The licking action of the mother should bring this plug out of the rectum soon after birth. If Mom seems slack you can help by stroking the pup's stomach. When about one-half of the plug appears, take hold and pull it gently, straight out.

The pups must have a chance to nurse for their fluid and be kept warm. One general rule, however, is to always keep the pups near the bitch's head so she can see them and tend to them.

The **colostrum**, or first milk the puppies drink, is important to their health. It is high in vitamins A and D and carries with it antibodies against diseases for which the bitch has been immunized. It is also a laxative and helps get the pups' little bodies to function normally.

If you should have a pup that is having difficulty breathing, hold it firmly in a towel, head slightly down, and swoop it in a head-to-knee movement. You are trying to empty the liquid from the nostrils and mouth. Do this several times, making sure to support the head and neck with the pup lying on its back.

Between puppies do put the delivered babies on the bitch's nipples. This makes the bitch relax and feel secure. When it looks like another puppy is on its way, remove the delivered ones to their warm box near the bitch's head.

After a long time with no straining or panting and no puppies, the whelping *could* be over, but the bitch will need the veterinarian's attention to make sure. Your vet will most likely give her an injection to make the uterus contract and rid it of any fluids and retained afterbirth material. This injection of akytocin also stimulates the flow of milk. Normally, full lactation occurs in three days. Your veterinarian also may want to give the new mother an antibiotic to ensure against uterine infection and, of course, go over the new litter to see that all are healthy.

CONCLUSION

You should let your veterinarian know ahead of time the approximate dates the pups are expected. You may want to call when the bitch actually goes into *active* labor so your veterinarian will be available if needed.

Be sure to ask the vet what to do if a pup is born seemingly lifeless, or how to help if a pup, even though being born normally, gets stuck in the birth canal. Do not confuse this with a pup who may be positioned incorrectly in the birth canal. This is a job for the veterinarian. Never try to reach into the birth canal for any reason.

Now that you have seen your bitch through a normal birth, you should be aware of signs to look for in an abnormal one. It is always a good idea to call your veterinarian if the bitch is:

1. Having strong, visible contractions more than twenty to thirty minutes before producing a pup.
2. In excessive pain.
3. Doing excessive straining.
4. Trembling or shivering, with cold extremities.
5. In collapse and exhaustion.
6. Vomiting.
7. Depressed after starting labor.
8. Having weak, infrequent, nonproductive contractions that fail to produce a pup within two to three hours.
9. Experiencing more than four-hour intervals between pups.
10. In prolonged gestation (past sixty-seven to sixty-eight days). Be sure breeding dates are accurate.
11. Producing green, bloody, puslike discharge without pups.

Being prepared for these events just may help to prevent them from happening!

11

Your New Akita Litter—After the Whelping

NOW THAT THE WHELPING is over and mother and babies are doing well, check the room temperature and offer the bitch water and some soft food.

Look in on the happy family often during the first few hours. This is a pleasurable task and important. Tiny as they are, puppies can wriggle away from the group and become chilled. There are always those strong puppies who dominate the milk bar and take away from the smaller or weaker pups. It's up to you to see that everyone has an equal chance.

Do not hesitate to handle the pups. They need to know the warmth of kind, human hands right from the start. Always *hold them gently but securely*. Hold them close to the mother's face so she will not become anxious.

Teach your children how to hold them *when the pups are*

159

older. Have them sit on the floor of the pen so there is no chance of a pup being dropped. Only do this if you have a bitch who is agreeable to it.

Be thoughtful of your bitch and don't bring the neighbors in to view the litter for at least three to four weeks. When you do invite them in, bring only one or two people at a time. Ask them to be quiet and stand at a distance. It's wise that first visitors be the persons the bitch knows well and likes. It's also good to eliminate those who own dogs. They could transmit disease to your pups. Precautions like these will help keep your pups' mortality rate low.

The pups' basic need for warmth and fluids will be met by the mother entirely for the first two weeks. After two weeks most pups can stand an air temperature of about 70 degrees F. Dampness and drafts are still to be avoided. A hand on a huddle of puppies should feel pleasantly warm. It is just as cruel to keep the pups in overheated conditions as to keep them cold. The room temperature at pen level should be your ever constant guideline.

Until the umbilical cords have dried up, check them daily and apply Betadine or tincture of iodine to the ends to aid in drying and prevent infection.

When the bitch is nursing, her diet will have to increase in respect to the pups' growth and demands for milk. Sometimes the bitch needs four times her normal amount. Therefore, it is wise to feed her several times a day. Her diet must have sufficient milk, meat, fat, fortified kibble and the vitamin supplement prescribed by your veterinarian. For the first few days she may be reluctant to leave her pups even for a few minutes. Feed her in the pen, lying down if she prefers. Pamper her. She deserves it.

THERE ARE PITFALLS

Now that you have found happiness in your warm puppies, we will warn you of some pitfalls. Rarely does everything go smoothly. Be prepared for the problems that could crop up.

Often, for some reason, puppies fade and die. Just as simple as that. Instead of gaining weight, they lose. This happens quickly, and unless you have baby scales and keep daily weight records,

160

you will have lost one puppy or more before you realize what is happening. A slight weight drop in the first day or two is not abnormal.

One to three ounces of weight gain per day is fairly average for an Akita puppy. If your pups are not gaining at this rate, perhaps they're not getting enough mother's milk.

Tenseness. Nerves. Diet. One of these might dry up the mother's milk. If you think you need to supplement, use a small baby bottle filled with formula for puppies. There are several excellent formulas on the market, one of which your vet may recommend. One **formula** that has been used with success follows:

	8 oz. homogenized milk
Equals 30	2 egg yolks
calories per oz.	1 tsp. corn oil
	1 drop multi-vitamin

Please note that the above formula for feeding is recommended to be given to each pup as follows:

First week—60–70 calories per lb. per day
Second week—70 calories per lb. per day
Third week—80–90 calories per lb. per day
Fourth week—100 calories per lb. per day

Instead of using the baby bottle to supplement, many breeders **tube feed**. If your vet suggests this method, be sure you know how to use it. Don't attempt it without the veterinarian demonstrating the method for you first. Use the tube *only* if a pup is too weak to **bottle feed**. You must stroke the puppy's genitals with a piece of cotton moistened with warm water to relieve it after feeding.

A puppy that appears to be in pain, struggling to relieve itself, may have impacted bowels. This condition has happened in puppies from something as simple as swallowing sand or pea gravel. A mild laxative or suppository recommended by your vet can relieve the situation that is causing the pup so much discomfort.

Viral infections and **bacterial disease** are more common than is usually realized, and are also a reason puppies fade. Frequent sterilization of feeding utensils is imperative. Milk is a breeding ground for bacteria. According to *The Complete Dog Book* by the

161

American Kennel Club (Howell Book House), mortality of young puppies may be as high as 20 percent to 30 percent per litter. This doesn't mean you will necessarily lose this many, but if you own a large kennel, that is what you can expect over a period of time.

Danger Signals

Watch your bitch carefully during the heavy nursing period, especially if she has a large litter. **Eclampsia**, a metabolic disorder involving the blood calcium level, may occur in bitches nursing or in late pregnancy. Several cases have been reported in the Akita breed. The first indication is extreme nervousness and rapid breathing. If she is not treated at once, the bitch will develop a stiff gait and seem to be under the influence of a martini or two. Within a short time she will fall and be rigid in appearance with intermittent severe muscle spasms. Then follows a period of convulsions which could lead to death.

Treatment should be immediate at the first signs of the condition. You can buy time by giving your bitch one adult-size, 5-grain aspirin tablet per ten pounds of body weight. The chemical action produced by the aspirin will cause a rapid rise in the blood's calcium level, but only temporarily. A veterinarian should be consulted immediately for intravenous calcium and supportive treatment.

This bitch is to be discouraged from further nursing. You will have to hand-nurse the litter. We suggest totally removing her from her litter until after each time the puppies have been tube fed or bottle fed.

Painful swelling or congestion of the breast can be relieved by allowing the puppies to nurse two or three times daily for ten to fifteen minutes each time. Camphorated oil, massaged into the breasts, will also help relieve the condition.

In most cases, eclampsia can be avoided by using a well-balanced diet throughout the pregnancy. Prenatal vitamin mineral supplement from last trimester through weaning is a must.

WEANING

Weaning puppies . . . how, when and with what is a very individual matter. No two breeders will agree 100 percent on all

EASTWIND'S MIA OF KOSHI-KI. Sire: Ch. Sakusaku's Steamboat Willie. Dam: Ch. Nan Chao's Hosi No Samurai. Owned by Ed and Marlene Sutton.

phases. Some people, after one litter, become instant experts! But the basic issue and the goal in the end are healthy puppies. After a number of years, many puppies, a lot of advice and some trial and error, all we can do is share general guidelines with you.

Some things become seemingly more haphazard now; note the word "seemingly." It's comparable to a recipe you've used for years. You no longer consult the cookbook, ingredients vary slightly and, if pressed for exact measurements, you look vague and mention pinches of "this and that," and say things like "it just looks right."

In general, the same thing applies to starting to wean a litter. If it's a small litter and Mama has plenty of milk, don't push the weaning. If it's a big litter and the bitch is low on milk or seems to be wearing down from the responsibilities of motherhood, then start once the pups are up on their feet and able to slurp out of a pan without falling in headfirst, at about three weeks.

Start with just one feeding a day. Increase the number of feedings rather rapidly. This is partly because of self-preservation. Sometimes it takes longer to clean up afterward than it takes for them to chow down. It's *hard* getting dried cereal out of small, fuzzy ears. Begin with a basic mixture of instant baby cereal (rice, oatmeal, hi-protein), a soft-moist dog food, condensed milk, some hamburger, all mixed with water and warmed up. Hamburger is a good "boost" in early puppy diets. Start them off by letting them lick the mixture off a finger, then put the finger into the dish, and pretty soon they get the idea, usually after they've walked through it a few times. Our experience has been that the condensed milk seems to sit better than either powdered milk or the bitch's milk substitutes. It has a good fat content and is easily digested. This is true even when you have a pup that has to have supplemental feedings by bottle or tube. At those times, add a little honey to condensed milk, some beef juice and vitamins recommended by your vet if this is the pup's main or only food supply.

As the pups increase in eating aptitude, increase the number of feedings, and start keeping the bitch away from them for longer periods of time. This progresses to the point where she can be away from them during the day but may sleep with them at night, to where she checks them out a couple of times a day so they get a few slurps, and then she gradually dries out.

Once the pups are able to manage more than the original mush, you can soak regular dog food in warm water and start mixing that in, cut down on the baby cereal gradually and start adding some regular canned meat. Begin decreasing the amount of moist-dry and condensed milk. Try not to let the pups get too roly-poly. It may look cute but is not the best thing for their growth and development.

As far as supplements go, *as long as the pups are getting some nourishment from mother, it is not necessary to start adding all kinds of vitamins and calcium.* As mentioned, let them continue to get some milk from mother as she begins to dry out. Sometimes there is a problem with bitches "pulling up" afterward, and a gradual, rather than an abrupt, withdrawal of mother's milk is to

164

be considered. Once they're on their own, give a good all-round vitamin and calcium, as recommended by your vet, in increasing amounts as the milk (canned or mother's) is decreased. In puppy foods made especially for growing youngsters where the vitamin and calcium content is greater than regular kibble, keep the supplements to a minimum. Try to *keep the diet simple*, and when the pup goes to a new home, include a list of what is fed, when and about how much. For some people, this may be their first purebred, probably their first Akita, and a puppy diet that's measured in milligrams of quarter-teaspoons will probably fall by the wayside with the new owner.

As stated in the beginning, there's a different formula for every breeder. The criteria for good, healthy pups: bright eyes, cold noses, shiny coats, weight increasing proportionate to size and, of course, good stools. Aside from being a good indication of good digestion and utilization of their food, anyone who has had eight or nine active pups rapidly gains a strong appreciation of good digestive function. So what you're working toward is a good basic diet with only enough supplementation to ensure good muscle and bone growth.

Also, if there's a problem that is not medical, a good, experienced breeder should be able to tell you more than a vet. This is not a put-down of veterinarians. Rely on yours and have confidence in them. We say this because vets deal primarily with illness or other medical problems, and not often with the numbers of litters or the day-to-day growth patterns that a good breeder of long standing has seen.

RECORD KEEPING

Finally, do keep records. This will aid you to evaluate growth patterns in your next litter, and can indicate early on if pups are not progressing as well as you'd like. It will also give you an eye for the puppies' development. You may recognize at some point one pup who is not quite up to snuff, but who, with a little supplementation, can catch up to and sometimes surpass littermates before any real problem develops.

WORMING AND CARE

Let us assume your bitch was wormed prior to conception and considered to be worm-free at the time of the puppies' birth. You still owe it to the buyers of your puppies to make sure roundworms or some other forms of parasite are not present in the pups. At approximately five weeks of age, take a stool sample from each pup to your vet. If parasites are detected, the veterinarian will either prescribe medicine or have you bring the pups in so that they can be cleaned out. It's a good idea to get a certificate stating either that the pups are free of parasites or the date worming took place. Every six months is a good rule of thumb for examining stool samples throughout a dog's life.

The most enjoyable part of raising puppies is watching them grow and develop. Try not to get too attached to any one pup and neglect the others. Give all of them the attention and human companionship they need at this crucial period of development. Try to spend at least fifteen minutes a day with each one, apart from the litter. Begin leash-breaking between six and seven weeks of age for short periods of time.

Make it a point each day to clean the whelping box and its tenants. Then spend some time grooming the bitch and wiping off the puppies if they look as if they could use it. By doing this on a daily basis, mother and her brood will feel secure. Eventually the wiping can turn into brushing, clipping the little nails and, in general, preparing them for grooming in their adult lives. For nails, use a pair of blunt-edged manicuring scissors, the kind sold for babies, as insurance against injury to bitch and each other.

Cleaning the whelping box is quite simple if you own three sections of indoor-outdoor carpeting the size of the box. Carpet can be hosed off and dries quickly. Most important, it provides a good surface for the pups to walk on. It's not slippery like newspapers. Consideration should be given to replacing the newspapers with the carpet or a nonskid material a day or two after whelping.

166

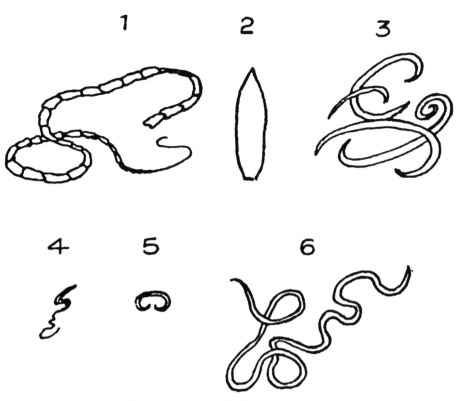

Types of worms: 1. Flea-host tapeworm; 2. Segment of tapeworm as seen in dog's stool; 3. Common roundworm; 4. Whipworm; 5. Hookworm; 6. Heartworm.

CULLING

To cull a litter is to make sure that those that are not up to par do not repeat their faults in progeny of their own. There are many reasons to consider culling. *We must assume that every person who breeds an Akita bitch or dog is interested in improving the quality of the breed as a whole.* As an individual concerned with the betterment of your breed, you must bear in mind what you would do if the following occurred:

A litter of seven puppies blessed your home. Two were marked much like Dalmatians, one had an overabundance of coat and one had a narrow pin head. The rest seemed to be lovely pups.

167

When you acquire an Akita puppy, like "Topsy," it just grows and grows. Pictured here is Am/Can Ch. SEAWOOD'S U.S.S. BUCKWHEAT, call name "Buck," at 5½ weeks of age. *Photo by Kelle.*

Am/Can Ch. SEAWOOD'S U.S.S. BUCKWHEAT pictured as an adult. Owned by Alyce and Kelle Clinton. *Photo by Kelle.*

168

You may decide to see what they look like when they are eight to ten weeks old. During this time it is not fair to the public or the breed to put this litter on the selling block. If, at the end of your waiting period, some of the pups are not up to the Standard for breed and not what you would want seen in the show ring, much less bred, it's up to you to do what will benefit the breed.

There are two ways of culling. Obviously defective pups may be put to sleep painlessly by a veterinarian shortly after birth. Or strictly pet-caliber animals may be placed in loving homes, sold with AKC limited registration and a written contract guaranteeing they will be spayed or castrated before they reach breeding age.

Culling is a touchy subject, but when you are striving for perfection for your breed, and when you realize that the world is already overcrowded with people and animals, there is a lot to be said in its defense.

REGISTERING AND SELLING THE PUPPIES

Now comes paperwork and heartbreak time. First, the paperwork. Register your litter with the American Kennel Club and prepare the individual forms sent to you for the new owners.

If there are puppies you feel should not be given full breeding registration (refer to section on culling), make sure your contract of sale includes this provision. In other words, have total agreement with your puppy buyers on the status of their new puppies in writing at time of sale.

Along with the registration papers, give each new owner:

- a sales receipt
- a health record
- a diet
- a contract detailing provisions of registration and/or sterilization agreements
- a manual for new puppy owners (a good idea)

Most important is a correct **pedigree**. It has come to our attention that some persons have received pedigrees containing incorrect spellings of dogs' names *and*, in some instances, the wrong ances-

NORTHLAND'S SNOW PANTHER, a five-month-old white male puppy with his owner, Christina Egland.

tors. A pedigree is like a birth certificate and should be treated as such. The names *must* be correct. There is no room for error in making them out.

The best interests of the breed and the public should take precedence over monetary gain to the breeder. Price your litter fairly, according to individual evaluation, and be consistent with the going rate of other purebred dogs of equal merit in your area. It's important to remember that when you set a high value on a pup and predict a glorious future for it, the buyer will usually hold you to the outcome you predict. For this reason it's wise to say to people about the pup they select, "This dog has show potential . . . *now*."

As any good breeder will tell you, determining a puppy's future ring status at age eight or ten weeks is a difficult thing to do.

After all of your wee prides and prejudices have left the nest, you must think of getting Mama's girlish figure back. While you can't ship her off to a health spa, you can cut back on her food intake. Make sure she has a balanced diet, plenty of exercise and keep her well groomed.

Within four months, with careful treatment, your Akita bitch can once again be the household treasure.

AKIHO headquarters and museum. Located in the remote northern part of Honshu Island, Akita Prefecture, the small city of Odate is host to the AKIHO organization, which administers to its 60-some branches throughout Japan and its one foreign branch in Los Angeles.

12

Specialty Clubs in the United States

THE AKITA CLUB OF AMERICA

The Akita Club of America is the Parent Club. Chapter 3, The Akita in America, covers its formative years.

In 1962, the club welcomed the Imperial Akita Club of Southern California into the fold as its first franchised chapter. Unfortunately, it was short-lived. The Eastern Akita Club, formed in 1963, was ACA's second chapter and remained intact until official AKC recognition of the breed.

In June 1964, the Parent Club presented more than 400 registrations, a Stud Book and assorted other documents to the American Kennel Club in a bid for recognition. However, in spite of this, AKC felt the time was not right for recognition and sent all records back to California.

Then, in 1969, ACA sponsored a symposium at the Anaheim Convention Center in Southern California. Dr. Frederick Pitts served as moderator. Joan Linderman was co-coordinator. A growing sophistication and thirst for knowledge among members drew a large audience. Club statistics showed that seven generations of Akitas had been bred in the United States. In 1969, 242 individual applications had been received for registration. That same year saw the founding of the Akita Rescue League, whose function it was to aid homeless Akitas. All chapters of the Parent Club were involved in an X-ray certification program for hip dysplasia. From this point on, the quest for recognition became an obsession with most Parent Club members.

The United States is divided into five regions by the Parent Club. Each region elects one representative to sit as a voting member on the Akita Club of America board of directors. Within these geographical regions are individual clubs, some of which are member clubs of the Akita Club of America. Member clubs have no direct connection with the regional representatives.

Regions

Northeastern, Region 1: Maine, New Hampshire, Vermont, Massachusetts, Rhode Island, Connecticut, New Jersey, New York, Pennsylvania, Ohio.

Southeastern & Southern, Region 2: Delaware, Maryland, Virginia, West Virginia, North Carolina, South Carolina, Georgia, Florida, Alabama, Tennessee, Kentucky, Mississippi, Missouri, Arkansas, Louisiana, Oklahoma, Texas.

North & South Central, Region 3: Indiana, Illinois, Michigan, Wisconsin, Iowa, North Dakota, South Dakota, Nebraska, Kansas, Montana, Wyoming, Colorado, New Mexico, Idaho, Utah, Arizona, Minnesota.

Western, Region 4: Alaska, Washington, Oregon, Nevada, Hawaii, Northern California (above a line parallel with Bakersfield).

Southern California, Region 5: All of California below a line parallel with the northern city limits of Bakersfield.

Member Clubs

Region 1
Greater Baltimore Akita Club, MD
Squakheag Akita Club, CT

A diorama of early Japanese hunters shows how native dogs, Akitas, and spears were used against the Japanese bear or yezo. This display is exhibited in the AKIHO museum.

O-Ken-In Akita Club, OH
Frontier Akita Club, KY

Region 2
Lone Star Akita Club of Houston, TX
Akita Club of Tampa Bay, FL
Heart of Texas Akita Club, TX
Dogwood Akita Club, GA
Orange Blossom Akita Club, FL

Region 3
Akita Club of Illini Valley, IL
*Rocky Mountain Akita Club, Inc., CO
Sho-Me Akita Club of the Ozarks, MO
Squaw Peak Akita Club of Phoenix, AZ
Heart of America Akita Club, KS
Great Lakes Akita Club, IL
Land of Enchantment Akita Club, NM

*Denotes licensed club

Region 4
Akita Club of Las Vegas, NV
Akita Club of Puget Sound, WA
Gold Country Akita Club, CA
Golden Gate Akita Club, CA
Cascade Akita Club, OR
Greater Spokane Akita Club, WA

Region 5
Inland Empire Akita Club, CA
Akita Club by the Sea, CA
Channel Islands Akita Club, CA

Club Biographies

Squakheag Akita Club

Originally founded as the New England Akita Club, the name was changed to Squakheag to comply with AKC regulations. The original membership included Jim Hermance (Kobra's Akitas), whose Ch. Mer Prince Taksan-Go was the first New England champion, Barbra and Bill Walker (Yamakumo's Akitas), Marsha Greenberg, Harold and Lillian Harrison, Una Nichols (Indian Hy Akitas) and Jane Abbott. The club was incorporated in Massachusetts and for many years the membership was concentrated between Springfield and Northfield.

The club remains one of the oldest regional clubs and hosted the 1993 National Specialty.

Rocky Mountain Akita Club, Inc.

Licensed club of the American Kennel Club and the first member club of ACA in the continental U.S. to achieve this status. Founded in 1979. In 1992 was the first local Akita club to be licensed by AKC (copy of AKC March 3, 1992, letter attached). In 1993 this club held their 1st Annual RMAC Independent Specialty.

176

THE AMERICAN KENNEL CLUB

March 3, 1992

Joyce Emery, Secretary
Rocky Mountain Akita Club
12821 Josephine Court
Thornton, CO. 80241

Dear Ms. Emery:

Further to our January 16, 1992 letter, the representations submitted on behalf of the Rocky Mountain Akita Club have been reviewed.

We are pleased to inform you that our committee acted favorably on your request and the Rocky Mountain Akita Club has been approved for the holding of licensed championship point events.

In granting this approval, our records have been noted to reflect that your club's focal point of dog interests and activities is greater Denver and it is expected that your club will continue to develop and serve the Akita interests in this area.

We enclose a small supply of Show Applications, forms for the submission of the names and assignments of judges (in the event your club wishes to designate it's breed's classes at an all-breed show as its specialty, we are also enclosing copies of such application - the all-breed club would be responsible for the submission of the names and assignments of judges as well as the site diagram), several sheets of graph paper, a few Sweepstakes/Futurity Applications, Guide for... Dealing With Misconduct..., Dog Show Rules, Obedience Regulations, and Regulations for Junior Showmanship.

If we can be of any assistance, please feel free to contact this office.

Sincerely yours,

Fran Hunt
Club Relations

FH:ab

AKITAINU HOZONKAI

The Nisei Week Akita show, held in August 1969, spurred much interest among Akita fanciers in the Los Angeles area. With encouragement from AKIHO and Japanese judge Dr. K. Ogasawara, and with permission and aid from Japan, the only branch of Akitainu Hozonkai outside Japan was formed in Los Angeles, California.

First branch chairman was Walter Imai. His own and his official staff's contributions to the Akita breed were monumental. Their bulletins carried translations of historical documents as well as Standards and articles on the breed as they were received from Japan. AKIHO meetings were well attended. Photos, movies and slides illustrated the breed in Japan. A highlight in the lives of AKIHO branch members occurred some years ago when Kusumaru-Go, a Tokuyu winner, a dog designated as "Superior" in Japan, was presented to Walter Imai by Mr. and Mrs. Taro Matsuda, owners of one of the most prominent Akita kennels in Tokyo. The author had the privilege of visiting the Matsudas in their lovely home in Japan. Their hospitality was typical of the goodwill shown by all Akita people and others in that country.

Since 1970, the Nisei Week AKIHO show has been sponsored

Akita dog statuary—a family.

MIKASA-GO, Seiken male.

by the parent AKIHO club, which provides the judge for each of these events. That person not only judges the dogs but holds seminars that are a source of enrichment for fanciers starved for historical information about their breed.

It is felt that the Los Angeles Branch had its greatest moment when they shared the dedication of the new AKIHO Headquarters in Odate, Japan, with the Parent Club.

The building is truly a monument to the breed. Costing over $400,000, it is supported by its nearly sixty branch clubs. From the gigantic mosaic of Akita dogs in the lobby to the spacious conference rooms, to the huge walk-in vault for registrations and historical documents, to the third floor museum that depicts the evolution and history of the Akita breed, it is a masterpiece of design.

We are now into the 1990s. AKIHO, Los Angeles Branch,

still disseminates information, still holds its annual show and is still a credit to the Akita breed.

There are many who believe that the genes of a perfect or near-perfect Akita lie cradled in the Orient. Now that importation of the breed has resumed, we may well be one step closer to that goal.

13

Evolution of the Breed in Canada

THE FIRST AKITAS to step foot on Canadian soil were brought into Smithers, North Central British Columbia, in the late 1950s: a male by Dr. Jim Proctor, and a female by Ed Carder.

Jerry and Sheryl Langan bought their first Akita from this pair's first litter, whelped in 1960. In February 1969, the Langans brought in Akita Tani's Empress Akiko from California.

Sonia Sitz and Kaye Otsuka came into contact with some American breeders and purchased the male puppy Nikko No Nikka Yuken. Gary and Joy Kennedy were next to purchase a female pup from the States. It would be correct to say that the evolution of the Akita breed in Canada began in the west.

According to Vera Bohac, former president of the Akita Club of Canada, to the best of her knowledge the first Akitas in Eastern Canada were those owned by Dr. Ted Thomas during the early 1970s. Shortly thereafter, Dr. Gary Seawright brought his Akitas to Canada from the United States, and jointly, with Dr. Thomas, began breeding them.

Am/Can Ch. DAVOS RONALD MACDONALD owned by Doctors Andy and Sheilah Fletch of Ontario. Sire: Ch. Sakusaku's Goro, Dam: Ch. Davos Choo Choo.

Several of Canada's early Akitas were registered with the Akita Club of America, but were *not* recognized by the American Kennel Club or the Canadian Kennel Club, so they could not be shown in official classes and could not be registered.

THE CANADIAN PARENT CLUB

A common goal brought the first Akita owners together to form a club. On April 16, 1972, in Lethbridge, Alberta, at an historic meeting, Sonia Sitz, Kaye Otsuka and Gary and Joy Kennedy formed the Akita Club of Canada. Several months of hard work produced a constitution and by-laws. In October 1972, the club was recognized by the Canadian Kennel Club. To achieve

MEGAMI, an early Japanese import. This wonderful red bitch has produced some amazing dogs for the Langan kennel.

		Toshiko
	Tora-Go	Koman Na Eiyu-Go
Megami (import)		Brandy Wine-Go
	Shasta-Go	Tenrai-Go
		Zoge Megami-Go

recognition of the breed, two major requirements had to be fulfilled: The breed Standard had to be written and approved and twenty-five purebred Akitas had to be registered. There were some other formalities that had to be completed as well.

Akitas made their first "unofficial" appearance in show rings in Canada in June 1972, when the first Akita with a transit pass

Ch. LANGAN'S AKA O'KASHII. This flashy red bitch with white mask was sired by Am/Can Ch. Toshiro's Karate Drift X the red import Megami.

Am/Can. Ch. TOSHIRO'S KARATE DRIFT, ROM. This male, owned by Sheryl Langan, was equally well known in the United States. He was also an American champion and is listed in the ROM section, having at least eleven champion offspring.

		Triple K Shogo
	Kinsei Suna Osama	
		Triple K Ginsei Shimo
Am/Can Ch. Triple K Tomo Go, ROM		
		Triple K Kenbo
	Nakkusu's Tamiko	
		Nakkusu's Miyoko
		Tochi Kumo-Go (a.k.a. "Gumo")
	Kumozakura	
		Byaku Ran Nyo-Go
Koinu		
		Toryu-Go
	Toshiro	
		Triple K Yoko

185

was shown at the Calgary Kennel Club show. This was Sonia Sitz's male, Nikko No Nikka Yuken.

In January 1973, Akitas were able to compete in the Miscellaneous Class. A month later, two Akitas were shown at the Alberta Kennel Club show in Calgary. They were Nikka and the Kennedy's female, Kyoko. The dogs were formally introduced to then-president of the Canadian Kennel Club, Hilda Pugh, to the Canadian Kennel Club representative and to the public.

In July 1973, Sheryl Langan's Tani's Empress Akiko won Best of Breed and first in Miscellaneous Class at Prince George, British Columbia. In that same month, at Millarville, Alberta, Dianne Wagner's Akita Tani's Kita placed Best of Breed and third in Miscellaneous Class. Thus the Akita started a whirlwind courtship with Canadian fanciers.

The Stud Book was set up in duplicate by Kaye Otsuka and submitted to the Canadian Kennel Club in August 1974. The breed Standard was written and the magic number of twenty-five dogs was finally reached. With pleasure, Sonia Sitz announced in the October 1974 issue of *Tayori*, the publication of the Akita Club of Canada, as unofficial news from the Canadian Kennel Club that the Akita would be recognized as of January 1, 1975. It was a dream come true. The original creators of the club, headed by Sonia Sitz, deserve full credit for the recognition of the Akita breed in Canada.

After breed recognition, the first Akitas to be shown in official classes were in Calgary, in January 1975. They were three littermates from the first Canadian registered litter, produced by Dianne Wagner, Daiken Akitas. Shortly thereafter, in March 1975, the first Canadian champion Akita was named. It was Kenjiko Royal Tenji. Vera Bohac's bitch, Daiken No Sakura, became the first female Canadian-born champion in June 1975.

As the breed's popularity thrived in Canada, the club also grew. With this growth came the inevitable problems that often accompany change. These problems were gradually settled and a new step in the club's evolution began. The club, which once centered in Western Canada, has now spread over the whole nation. Provincial representatives were appointed for each province and became liaisons between the club officials and members all over the country. The official newsletter, *Tayori*, was upgraded and served as the main communication within the club. It is in this way that the members were kept informed and involved in club activities.

EARLY FIRSTS

During 1977, the Akita Club of Canada organized the first Canadian Akita booster show, which was held in Lethbridge, Alberta, on April 16. Ch. Checan's Subarashii Checan, owned by Vera Bohac, was the winner. The same year also saw the first Akita go Best in Show. Ch. Gin Gin Haiyaku-Go of Sakusaku, CACIB, garnered the award at St. Francis Kennel Club show, Bromont, Quebec, on July 1, under judge John Stanek.

Canadian-born Ch. Langan's Amaterasu O-Mi-Kami, owned by the Russels, was the first Best Puppy in Show in Canada. The first Obedience title was received by a Canadian-bred male, Daiken's No Kuro Kuma. He was trained by co-owner Constable Barry Bell of the Royal Canadian Mounted Police. Daiken's No Kuro Kuma was co-owned by his breeder, Dianne Wagner of Hague.

The Akita Club of Canada's standing objectives are to protect and promote the breed, prevent crossbreedings and provide information, knowledge and education so that the public may come to know this wonderful breed as a loyal friend of all people.

THE CANADIAN BREED STANDARD

The Revised Standard for the Akita Breed as Approved at the February 19, 1975, Meeting of the Board of Directors of the Canadian Kennel Club

1. *Origin and Purpose:*

The Akita, whose history dates back some 300 years, derives its name from the Prefecture of Akita, in northern Japan. At one time, in the early days of the breed, Akitas were considered a national treasure and only nobles could own one. In 1931, this

The first Best in Show Akita in Canada was the Am/Can Ch. GIN-GIN HAIYAKU-GO OF SAKUSAKU in Quebec, 1977.

Am/Can Ch. YAMAKUMO'S ITAZURA SAMA won the first Canadian National Specialty handled by owner Barbara Walker. Sama was a multiple Group winner, number one Akita in Canada for four years and was the sire of a Best in Show dog.

beautiful dog was proclaimed a natural monument by the Japanese Ministry of Education, and the government took all necessary steps to preserve the breed. The Akita is primarily a working dog and has been used for guard work, a guide for the blind, a protector of children and home, a hunting companion and sled work.

2. *General Appearance:*

Large, powerful, alert, with much substance and heavy bone, the broad head, forming a blunt triangle, with deep muzzle, small eyes and erect ears carried forward in line with back of neck, is characteristic of the breed. The large, curled tail, balancing the broad head, is also a characteristic of the breed.

189

3. *Temperament:*

Alert and responsive, dignified and reserved, but courageous, friendly toward people and often aggressive toward other dogs. The Akita barks infrequently and then only as a warning signal. The demeanor suggests activity and agility.

4. *Size:*

Height: Dogs 26 inches or more at the shoulder, bitches 24 inches or more at the shoulder. The male's body length to height ratio is approximately 10:9 and the female slightly greater. The dog is powerfully built, with bone and substance proportionate to height.

5. *Size and Colour:*

Double-coated. Undercoat soft and very dense and shorter than outercoat. Outercoat straight, harsh and standing somewhat off body. Hair on head, legs and ears short. Length of hair at withers and rump approximately 2 inches, which is slightly longer than the rest of body except tail, where coat is longest and most profuse. Any colour, brindle, white (no mask) or pinto. Colours are brilliant and clear and markings are well balanced, with or without mask or blaze. Pinto has a white background with large, evenly placed patches covering head and more than one-third of body. Undercoat may be a different colour from outercoat. The white Akita should have pigmented eyes, dark nose and lips.

6. *Head:*

a) Skull—massive but in balance with the body, tending to be flat on top, with the rest of the head forming a blunt triangle when viewed from top, free from excessive wrinkle when at ease, median fissure clearly visible and stop well defined.

b) Muzzle—broad and full, distance from nose to stop is the distance from stop to occiput as two is to three.

c) Nose—broad and black, liver nose permitted on light Akitas but black always preferred.

190

d) Mouth—clean, powerful jaws, lips black and heavy but not pendulous, tongue pink, teeth strong with scissor bite preferred but level bite acceptable.

e) Eyes—dark brown, small, deep-set and triangular in shape, eye rims black and tight.

f) Ears—the ears of the Akita are characteristic of the breed. They are strongly erect and small in relation to rest of head. If ear is folded forward for measuring length, tip will touch upper eye rim. Ears are triangular, slightly rounded at tip, wide at base, set wide on head but not too low and carried slightly forward over eyes in line with back of neck.

7. *Neck:*

The neck is thick and muscular; comparatively short, widening gradually toward shoulders. A pronounced crest blends in with base of skull.

8. *Forequarters:*

a) Shoulders—strong and powerful with moderate layback.

b) Upper arm—heavy-boned and straight as viewed from front. Elbows neither turning in nor out.

c) Lower arm—heavy-boned and straight as viewed from front. Dewclaws generally not removed.

d) Pasterns—angle of pastern 15 degrees from vertical.

e) Feet—cat feet, well-knuckled up with thick pads. Feet straight ahead.

9. *Body:*

a) Topline—level back.

b) Chest—is wide and deep; depth of chest is one-half height of dog at shoulder. Ribs well sprung, brisket well developed.

c) Loin—firmly muscled and moderate tuckup.

d) Croup—slightly rounded.

e) Abdomen—is drawn up and tucked up.

10. *Hindquarters:*

a) Hipbone—width, muscular development and bone comparable to forequarters.

b) Upper Thigh—well developed and powerful.

c) Lower Thigh—should be comparable to forequarters. Dewclaws permissible.

d) Hocks—less angular than many breeds 145 to 160 degrees, turning neither in nor out.

e) Stifle Bend—stifle is moderately bent.

f) Feet—same as front.

11. *Tail:*

Large and full, set high and carried over back or against flank in a three-quarter, full or double curl, always dipping to or below level of back. On a three-quarter curl, tip drops well down flank. Root large and strong. Tail reaches hock when let down. Hair coarse, straight and full, with no appearance of a plume.

12. *Gait:*

Brisk and powerful with strides of moderate length. Back remains strong, firm and level. Rear legs move in line with front legs.

Faults:

1. Narrow or snipy head
2. Round or light eyes
3. Excessive dewlap
4. Light bone, rangy body
5. Elbows in or out, loose shoulders
6. Indication of ruff or feathering of coat
7. Coarseness in bitches
8. Overrefinement in males

192

Disqualifications:

1. Monorchids or cryptorchids
2. Viciousness, instability
3. Excessively overshot or undershot
4. Albinos
5. Pink noses, eyelids or rims, butterfly nose
6. Uncurled tail
7. Drop or broken ears
8. Deafness
9. Excessive entropion or ectropion
10. Altering a coat or general appearance by scissoring or clipping

Scale of Points

(1)	General appearance	20
(2)	Characteristic	10
(3)	Head	20
(4)	Back, Fore and Hindquarters	10
(5)	Chest and Abdomen	10
(6)	Members, Feet and Soles	10
(7)	Coat	10
(8)	Gait, Pace	10
	TOTAL	100

A SPECIAL DOG IN CANADA

We can think of no better way to conclude this chapter than to share with you some memories of Sheryl Langan's, which suggest that the Akita's early heritage and instincts come to the fore with each passing generation.

Neh-Wa's Story

This Akita pup always caught everyone's eyes and had a boldness about him that was surprising in a pup so young. While still a baby, Neh-wa came down with hepatitis, which nearly cost him

NEH-WA

his life. After a long battle he recovered but was left with minor problems that reoccurred for the remainder of his life. Memories of Neh-wa as a puppy were typical of most Akitas, but at the time our knowledge of the breed was limited. His habits of keeping clean, enjoying high places and never once having an accident in the house were all very unique to us.

Neh-wa grew into a very impressive animal. He stood 27 inches at the withers and when in top shape weighed 140 pounds. He had a coal-black coat when young, and in later years the hair around his neck turned a rusty black. His head was massive and extremely bearlike. He had a tightly curled tail and a gait that would put a good trotting horse to shame.

194

Neh-wa grew up around all types of farm and ranch animals, loving and protecting them all. His natural instinct as a guard dog came to the fore, using that deep Akita bark to ward off intruders to his property. Most of our visitors would wait politely in their cars until we came to escort them past Neh-wa. He was never mean or vicious, but demanded respect from outsiders. After our visitors were properly introduced, Neh-wa would tolerate them.

In the cattle business a good dog can save an owner a lot of steps and Neh-wa took to this work naturally. We could leave gates open with Neh-wa stationed at the entrance, and he would not let one cow slip by, although try they did! He would flush mavericks (stray cattle) out of the dense brush where our horses could not go. Yet he really liked the cattle and horses and many times would babysit newborn calves and foals. He would also keep the range cows occupied and away from us while we treated or marked their calves.

We were not bothered much by predators; however, around breakup, coyotes would close in near calving time. Calving season was an important time of year, so several times during the night and early morning we would check the maternity area. In one particular instance a heifer wandered from the main bunch to calve. Neh-wa was on patrol when three coyotes were headed toward the laboring cow. Neh-wa stalked the coyotes, then moved in like a panther. He killed one coyote on the run, and the second was badly wounded, while the third managed to get away by the skin of his teeth. Stray dogs received the same treatment and stayed clear of the ranch.

Along with the cattle, we operated a guide outfitting business in the fall. We packed into some of toughest country imaginable. Neh-wa loved these trips and would walk and trot the long rough 50 miles to our first base camp. He was mostly with us just for the outing but always felt very important if he was allowed to track a wounded animal. He of course enjoyed keeping the numerous camp robbers and whiskey jacks out of the camp, which provided endless amusement for our hunters.

We all had many experiences, some good and some bad, up in the mountains. One occasion I still recall as vividly as the day it happened was Neh-wa's encounter with the "wolverines," (unholy terrors of the wilds). We had left our base camp with a group of photographers who wanted to shoot pictures of the elusive mountain goats. Jerry, Neh-wa and I had gone ahead on a scouting trip over some jagged, rough terrain. Neh-wa was the first to spot a couple of nannies and their two youngsters. They were peacefully eating moss along rocky ledges.

We watched them for a while and were about to go back for the photographers when Neh-wa started to grumble deep in his throat, and then off he went down the shalelike ledge. We both stood up and saw the trouble. Two full-grown wolverines were stalking the young goats. We called Neh-wa back but it was too late; he had attacked the larger wolverine from behind. The smaller of the two took one look at Neh-wa, then us, and he took off. The larger wolverine, furious and snarling, fought hard. Knowing the wolverine's reputation, we thought Neh-wa was a goner. However, quick and agile as a cat himself, Neh-wa escaped most of the wolverine's vicious assaults. We came in closer. Maybe it was our presence, but the two separated long enough for Jerry to get a shot at the wolverine. Neh-wa watched the carcass for a few minutes until he was satisfied it was dead. Then we attended to Neh-wa's wounds. Neh-wa had done his job and protected the goats just like the farm animals at home. Most dogs have a natural fear of a wolverine and with good reason. It is noted for ferocity, strength and nasty temper, allowing the wolverine virtually no enemies.

Neh-wa's fame as a good bush dog was well known and the local detachment of RCMP, who had no dogs of their own, borrowed our big black Akita to find lost hunters. One lost soul has been an Akita fan ever since.

As a bird dog in the thick-tangled bush of Smithers, British Columbia, Neh-wa was exceptional. He retrieved very well and never damaged a bird. We usually hunted ruffed grouse or blue grouse, but retrieving them in brush without a good bird dog would have resulted in many lost birds.

Neh-wa was Obedience-trained and did a fair share of parlor tricks. He was always a ''ham'' and really performed for company. He also loved having his picture taken and would pose like a statue looking very dignified, but as soon as he heard the camera shutter click, he was off.

If Neh-wa was fond of a person, member of the family or family friend, he would take them for walks holding their hands gently in his mouth. If Neh-wa wanted to show someone something, he would do the same thing. He would silently glare at people he did not like or trust, giving them his most disdainful look. Neh-wa's judgment of people was exceptionally keen. He also did not like people to drink and would growl at them or just give them the "eye."

In later years he learned to pull a sled and became extremely adept. A special nylon backpack was made, thus allowing him to carry his own food on our excursions into the back country.

In time we sold our cattle business and began raising Arabian horses. We had visitors from all over the country dropping by our ranch, and many were just as interested in our strange "bear dog" as in the aristocratic Arabians. Some of our visitors had seen Akitas in the United States or Japan and convinced us we should raise Akitas as well. But where to find a good Akita bitch was the question. After two years of searching we finally found a breeder in California and purchased a pretty red-fawn female with black mask. We also bought a Kuro-Goma male pup and were happy with both puppies. Neh-wa liked the pups and helped to raise them. We were very much looking forward to the day when we could raise our own Neh-was. However, Neh-wa's earlier case of hepatitis had left him incapable of producing puppies. Needless to say we were all very disappointed.

Neh-wa suffered a lot in the final year of his life with reoc-curring bouts of urinary tract infections. During this last year in 1974 we sold our ranch in British Columbia and bought our present Driftwood Ranch in Goodfare, Alberta. Trying to move a whole ranch with over forty head of registered horses, farm equipment, household belongings and three adult Akitas was quite an undertaking. Neh-wa seemed ready for the new adventure and was bright-eyed and alert the whole way. He reigned supreme over the other two Akitas and barked at any curious passersby or service station attendants.

Upon arrival at our new ranch, Neh-wa made the rounds and established his new territory. The excitement and change was a little too much for the proud old dog who was now fourteen years of age. A short three weeks later we lost him. We buried him at a special place on the ranch overlooking our marsh lake, which is the annual resting grounds for Canada geese and other waterfowl. As he always loved helpless birds and animals, we felt he would be happy there. We think he is.

Neh-wa will always have a soft spot in our hearts. Our memories of this wonderful, proud dog are too numerous to chronicle. The saying "The Akita possesses the heart of a lion, the look of a bear and the agility of a cat" is definitely true of our Neh-wa.

This is your story, Neh-wa. We hope you approve.

14

Specialty Shows and Events—Before and After AKC Recognition

Some of our early breeders and exhibitors of Akitas had never owned another breed of dog before this Japanese import captured their fancy. Most were novices and unfamiliar with the breed.

Shortly after the Akita's initial influx into the United States, in 1956, access was gained to the American Kennel Club show rings via the Miscellaneous Class. Hardly a judge, exhibitor or spectator knew which of many types was correct.

This is a most important chapter. It will show the way Specialties dictate or force a breed to go in various directions, some frequently contradictory to the Standard. Novices with bitches to be bred sometimes go to the big winner of the day. Top winning males often do not produce as good as they are themselves. It is, therefore, imperative you study the text and pictures in this chapter and research pedigrees as carefully as possible.

Reminisce with us down the long trail of all-Akita gatherings that represent our Specialities and all-breed events both before and after AKC recognition of our breed. From 1955 to the present day, our journey will wend its way through this chapter. Who knows? We may all profit from a little reviewing of what we have done to and with our beloved breed, the Akita.

The owners of this country's "new breed" were so encouraged by the American Kennel Club granting them the right to exhibit their dogs in the Miscellaneous Class on July 13, 1955, that the opportunity to gather in groups was beginning. Akita owners were "hooked" after Homare No Maiku-Go was awarded the prized First Place Miscellaneous Class ribbon by judge Marie B. Myer on January, 1956, at the Orange Empire show in California. According to records, there were twenty-one licensed shows in which a total of thirteen Akitas were shown in 1956.

THE FIRST SPECIALTY SHOWS

The year was 1959. An informal group of twenty-two Akitas and owners gathered in front of a kennel in Van Nuys, California. That it *did* happen, and our breed had gathered together for a time of comparison is important, but we can only consider this a beginning. The hub of Akitadom and many of the breed's greatest supporters were then situated in the Southern California area. From there came the urge to display the breed in great numbers. Thus came about the first all-Akita show in 1960, sponsored by the **Akita Club of America**, with its membership of eighty-seven.

A catalog featuring the lovely bitch Silver Crown Momo on its cover contained the names of twenty-eight entries. The judge was the well-known terrier handler and now multi-group judge Rick Chasoudian, who had been briefly exposed to the breed in Japan when he served with the U.S. Army.

A few now-familiar names and faces were there with their

early Akitas: Al and Liz Harrell of Akita Tani, Ben, Walter and Camille Kam of Triple K and Bert and Nancy Hoeltje of Koyama and Anne Powell of Oshio. Fading slowly out of the Akita game as new fanciers came in were such names as Fisher, Wondries, Conway, Noble, Strader, Lucas, Brown and Greber. Yet they are names to be remembered as they had set patterns for the breed in its early stages in the United States.

Best of Breed was Ben Kam's import bitch, Fukuchiyo-Go, who was brought into this country with her kennel mate, Goroni-shiki-Go, by the Kams: Walter, who was then in the U.S. Navy, Ben, the father, and young Camille. Best of Opposite Sex went to Lee and Janet Fisher's imported male, Homare No Maiku-Go, the same male who had won the first Miscellaneous Class in 1956.

April 16, 1961, was the date and Waller Park, Santa Maria, California, the setting for Akita Club of America's second annual event. Forty Akitas were entered. Dr. W. Creamer of Pasadena, California, judged Japanese Ch. Fuji Akashi-Go, owned by M/Sgt. B. J. Arlen as Best of Breed, with Fukuchiyo-Go as Best of Opposite Sex.

The third annual all-Akita Specialty was held in Fontana in 1962. Ruth McCourt judged. Lillian Koehler, wife of Bill Koehler of Obedience fame, was the ring steward. This time, Best of Breed went to Kuroi Yoru No Akita Ken, owned by the late Anita Powell, Oshio Ken kennel. Anita, who had spent much time in Japan earlier, had tremendous insight as to what the Akita was in Japan in those days. Her information was not secondhand. Her awareness for a typey Akita was to be respected. Best of Opposite Sex went to a young bitch from the 6 to 9 Month Class, Triple K Ginsei Shimo, owned by William Conway. She was later to become better known through her son, the winning Mex. Ch. Kinsei Suna Nihon-no Taishi, CD, owned by Dr. Joseph Vogl.

All over the U.S., 1963 was an active year for the breed. On the East Coast, Lil O'Shea and her Shiroi O'Sama-Go, better known as "White King-Go," were winners at the Lady and the Dog parade in Rittenhouse Square, Philadelphia.

On the West Coast, the fourth annual Akita show brought approximately fifty Akitas, with Vincent Perry officiating at Reseda Park in the San Fernando Valley, on October 13. Dokakoku-No

Akita Ken was Best of Breed. He was owned by Neil Noble. Born October 20, 1959, at Akita Ken kennel, his sire was Kuromen of Akita Ken, his dam, Yonaka Tsuki of Akita Ken. Best of Opposite Sex, once again, was Fukuchiyo-Go of the Triple K kennel.

This was also a good year for the Akitas in the American Kennel Club Miscellaneous Class. The late Louis J. Murr judged twenty-five dogs and twenty-five bitches at the old **Harbor Cities Kennel Club** show at Long Beach, California, in June. It was the biggest entry to date. First place went to Triple K Hayai Taka, who seemed to be following the winning path of his mother, Fukuchiyo-Go. First-place bitch was the lovely Triple K Ginsei Shimo, back in the limelight again.

In 1964, Liz and Al Harrell produced a winning specimen in their breeding program in Akita Tani's Shoyo-Go. Shoyo became the pillar behind the Akita Tani kennel. It was on this dog and his offspring that the Harrells truly established themselves on the West Coast. Wade Chandler, another Akita owner, handled the big boy to his first win under Major B. Godsol, at the Harbor Cities Kennel Club fixture in Long Beach, California. There were thirty Akitas present in Miscellaneous. This win proved to be the first of quite a few to follow for Shoyo in the Miscellaneous ring.

The Akita Club of America's fifth annual event, in 1964, found the bitch from the 12 to 14 Month Class, Michiko of Oshio Ken, bred by Anita Powell and owned by J. R. Taylor, winning Best of Breed. Edward Hirschman officiated at this fixture, which once again was held in Reseda Park.

Still in 1964, the **American Akita Breeders**, a splinter group from the Akita Club of America, brought Mr. M. Wakisaka from Japan to do the honors in the ring. Best of Breed was the import pinto dog, Hozan, owned by Ivan Wong. Once again, Best of Opposite Sex went to Triple K Ginsei Shimo.

Hozan consistently won during his brief show career under American judges. It would seem, while not using the identical Standards as a guide, at that time judges from both America and Japan did end up agreeing on what dogs were to be placed at the head of the class.

A lovely cream-colored bitch, Ichiban Shanpan, bred by Mr. and Mrs. R. Judd and Mrs. Judd's sister, Nancy Hoeltje, was starting what was to become an outstanding show career in the Miscellaneous class. Shan was top winning Akita in the United States for 1965 and 1966. She left the Akita breeding world some good progeny.

The sixth annual Akita Club of America show was held in Anaheim, California, in December 1965, with an approximate entry of fifty. The all-white Rikimaru-Go, owned by Tad Yamaoka, went Best of Breed under judge Roy Henre of Jet kennel. Riki's name was duly engraved on the club's perpetual Japan Airlines trophy. A good-sized dog with a charming personality and sparkling coat, he was a good choice. To fanciers, the impact of a white Akita winning was stunning. Best of Opposite Sex was the Harrell's Parnassus Meiyo of Akita Tani.

In Ensenada, Mexico, where official Akita championships could be earned, Triple K Hayai Taka and Triple K Shina Ningyo became the first and second Akita champions. The show was a distant form of recognition for the breed under show conditions. Needless to say, Taka and Shina's owners, Camille Kam and her mother, Emma Jung, were elated at the win.

In the meantime, the American Akita Breeders, in one of their early match shows in 1966, had judges from Japan. Famed AKIHO judge, Dr. Shinichi Ichiguro, a veterinarian, and Mr. Hiroshi Abe, longtime Akita breeder and fancier, did the honors.

With both clubs holding shows, the Akita had the ring exposure necessary to develop the breed and work toward American Kennel Club recognition. With an entry of seventy-three, the Akita Club of America's seventh annual Specialty show, judged by C. L. Savage, saw Glenn and Gloria Bearss' twenty-two-month-old Akita Tani's Toyo Koshaku win Best of Breed in November 1966. Best of Opposite Sex honors went to an eleven-month-old bitch, Nakusso's Ginko, owned by Mr. and Mrs. David Ross. Ginko went on to some fine wins in her show career.

This was the first show given by the **Akita Club of America** that included **Obedience**. A brilliant exhibition was put on by Joe Vogl and his Triple K Kiyomi, CD. Kiyomi, an outstanding bitch in the Obedience ring, did Recalls that would have been a credit to any breed.

It was a busy year. The Akita Club of America held its third annual puppy match at La Palma Park in Anaheim. Judge Leo

Rifkind, DVM, had forty-eight Akita puppies to choose from. Best Puppy was Triple K Miko, a pretty pinto bitch owned by Dianne Russell, Fukumoto Akitas. Miko, sired by Mex. Ch. Triple K Hayai Taka out of Mex. Ch. Triple K Shina Ningyo, was shown impeccably. Later on, others would say she was bred to perfection when she was bred to Kinsei Suna Nihon No Taishi and produced Mex. & Am. Ch. Fukumoto's Ashibaya Kuma, ROM.

The American Akita Breeders provided ample shows in 1967 for the breed. At their spring show, a young bitch, Akita Uchi's Tomodachi-Go, sired by Akita Uchi's Tennotanjobi, won Best of Breed. Owned by Mr. and Mrs. William Belser, this animal showed a lot of Akita spunk and won hands down. Best of Opposite Sex was Triple K Haku, bred and owned by Camille Kam. Best of Breed Junior was a red dog, Tokubetsu Akai Inu, owned by Roy Cantrell. Best of Opposite Sex Junior went to a red-and-white pinto bitch, Sakusaku Gorotsuki-Go, owned by Joan and Susan Linderman.

There were 47 litters and 123 individual dogs registered with the Parent Club in 1967. Things were growing rapidly.

In 1968, the American Akita Breeders hosted another spring show, which drew seventy-eight entries. Judged by Svend Jensen, Best of Breed went to the often winning, dynamic Mex. Ch. Kinsei Suna Nihon-No Taishi, CD, owned by Dr. and Mrs. Joseph Vogl, with Best of Opposite Sex honors to Mex. Ch. Sakusaku Gorotsuki-Go. In this same show, Fukumoto's Ashibaya Kuma came from the 6 to 9 Month Class to go Best in Show Junior, following right behind his sire, Taishi.

Out of an entry of ninety, a grown-up Kuma captured Best of Breed at the Akita Club of America's ninth annual event on October 27, 1968. His dam, Triple K Miko, took Best of Opposite Sex. Though they did not resemble each other, they were an outstanding pair at the time. Veteran Bitch, first place, owned and handled by Camille Kam Wong, was Jimars Sakura of Triple K, litter sister to Jimars Hikari of Maru, dam of Ichiban Shanpan and Ichiban Mitsubachi, CD. Best of Breed Junior went to Tamiko, owned by Mr. Ely, who was shown in the 9 to 12 Month Class.

In that same show, other youngsters who were destined to make a tremendous impact on the Akita breed in the future were

Sakusaku's Tom Cat-Go, Sakusaku's Tiger Lily, Akita Tani's Kuro-yama, Imperial Fuji-Hime, Akita Tani's Sakatumi, to name a few.

This same year was distinguished by the **Midwestern Akita Club's** first show. Best of Breed went to Gary Seawright's Silver Crown Mata and Best of Opposite Sex to Ben Tomazewski's Katsu Akita Tano.

On November 10, 1968, there were seventy-eight Akitas to choose from at the American Akita Breeders fall fixture. A winning combination that was to repeat itself at a later date was Best of Breed Fukumoto's Ashibaya Kuma, owned by Harold Hunt, and Best of Opposite Sex Parnassus Meiyo of Akita Tani, owned by Al and Liz Harrell.

It is interesting to note that 233 individual Akitas were registered with the Parent Club in 1968.

A banner show year for the breed was 1969. In Los Angeles, in the heart of Little Tokyo, the annual **Nisei Week Festival** took place. For the first time, and because of the dedication of many Akita fanciers, an all-Akita show was included in the program. AKIHO judge Dr. Kinichi Ogasawara was flown in from Japan. Amid much pomp and ceremony and from the largest entry of Akitas ever assembled at one show in the United States (136), the young brindle bitch, Sakusaku's Tiger Lily, handled by Susan Linderman Sanett, was chosen for Best of Breed. It is to be noted that Tiger Lily was out of two recent imports that were to become most important to the breed.

Registration of Akitas rose again in 1969, with 64 litters registered and 242 individual registrations. At this date seven generations of Akitas had been bred in the United States and it often seemed like they were all in the show ring. This year was indeed significant. It made deep inroads into the approach to recognition for the breed.

The American Akita Breeders and the Akita Club of America were not sitting still in 1969. Once again the big gray Fukumoto's Ashibaya Kuma went Best of Breed at the ACA annual May show and Best of Breed at the ACA annual Specialty. In an entry of ninety-six, Best of Opposite Sex went to Parnassus Meiyo of Akita Tani. Once again it should be mentioned that these two were not alike in type. Down through the years judges have been confused on the issue of Akita type, but no more so than many breeders.

The year 1970 started out with a great show put on by the young **Royal Akita Club of Northern California**. Judge Florence Savage had forty-six entries and for Best of Breed chose Akita Tani's Togo, owned by Mr. Brooke. Best of Opposite Sex was Akita Tani's Kokishen, owned by M. Steeves and Liz Harrell. First in the Open Bitch Class at this event was Sakusaku's Tiger Lily from Southern California. Second was her dam, Japanese Gr. Ch. Haruhime (Kito), owned by Barbara and Don Confer from Petaluma. This was one of the rare times Kito made a public appearance. She is well worth remembering as a major contributor to the breed. Her first litter produced such familiar names as Kabuki, Star, Tom Cat, Tiger Lily and Rowdy.

In May, the **Akita Fanciers of San Diego** had forty-four Akitas at their show. Judge Virginia Miller placed Tusko's Kabuki, then owned by J. Linderman, Best of Breed. R. Wright's Meyoshii garnered Best of Opposite Sex.

The Akita Club of America's annual Fall Specialty had an impressive 109 entered. Judge Stephen Hubbell awarded Mex. Ch. Fukumoto's Ashibaya Kuma Best of Breed and the Ross' Mex. Ch. Nakusso's Ginko Best of Opposite Sex. The young Triple K Tomo-Go was Best of Winners.

The Midwestern Akita Club saw brindle import Azuma Riki Maru, owned by Capt. Ken Mayhew, going Best of Breed at their Specialty.

By this time, the Nisei Week All-Akita show was ready for a second try at the world. The people involved had formed a dedicated organization that attempted to bridge the learning gap about the Akita breed between East and West. They were initially responsible for the wedding of the West Coast organizations into tentative peace and harmony that eventually, after many interruptions, led to AKC recognition. More about this in the chapter on clubs.

Total entry was 107. The Honorable Judge Mr. Hiraizumi officiated. Best of Breed was Triple K Chiyo, owned by Camille and Ben Kam, and Best of Opposite Sex was the big striped dog Sakusaku's Tom Cat-Go. Best of Breed Junior was Yuki, owned by Mr. Ikeda, and Best Opposite Junior was Kanpuzan, brought back from Northern Japan by J. Linderman.

In 1971, Sakusaku Gorotsuki-Go went Best of Breed at the

Royal Akita Club of Northern California's Specialty held at Pacifica. Judge Frank Abarta gave Tusko's Kabuki Best of Opposite Sex. The big red machine was just starting his show career and was to become the top Akita in America in 1972 on the Akita Club of America point system. He was then owned and handled by Pete Lagus.

At the annual Nisei Week show in August of 1971, Mr. Zenzo Watanabe from the AKIHO organization in Japan chose a typey brindle male for Best of Breed. Owned by Bob Shibasaki, Shinun-Go was in good form.

The fall of 1971 saw Jane Wilson's Kofuku-no's Chiisai Kuma, a bitch, take Best of Breed at the Midwestern Akita Club's fixture.

In 1972 the smell of recognition by the American Kennel Club permeated the air. The local club shows continued with an eye toward more professionalism in the hope it would aid the cause.

The Eastern Akita Club Specialty saw Barbara Miller's Sakura's Bushi, CD, win Best of Breed, while a youngster, Mitsu Kuma's Tora-Ojii-Go, owned by Lorea Wright, earned the Highest Score in Trial in Obedience competition. Both of these dogs went on to become champions upon recognition in 1973. Tora became one of the most consistent Best of Breed and Group-placing early winners on the East Coast. His record was enviable.

At the Royal Akita Club's third annual Specialty, Wanchan's Akagumo was Best of Breed and had his name engraved on the perpetual trophy alongside the name of Sakusaku Gorotsuki-Go and Akita Tani's Togo.

It was about this time that the authors of this book first met. In May 1972, at a match show put on by the Los Encinos Kennel Club in the San Fernando Valley of California, Virginia Funk judged Joan Linderman's young puppy "Diamond Lil" Best of Breed and her now famous "Chester" Best of Opposite Sex. Both dogs soared to great heights less than two years later. Sakusaku's Diamond Lil finished her championship twenty-three days after the breed was recognized. Undefeated in her sex, she had a record-breaking sixty-plus Bests of Breed to her credit, all won between 1973 and 1975. She produced such outstanding bitches as Ch. Ketket's The Primrose Path, Ch. Ketket's Dyn-O-Mite O'Sakusaku and Ch. Ketket's Tigger no Nan Chao, ROM, 1977's top winning Midwestern bitch.

Later in May, the Midwestern Akita Club Specialty Match top winners were Mr. Goldamer's Krug's Sotto, bred by Bettye Krug, with Best of Opposite Sex going to Richard and Emily Woods's Kuro Panzu Maru No Asagao. Richard had always handled his own dogs with great success and a real style of showmanship.

It was a busy year indeed in 1972. On August 13, Al Young's Tomoe Hime went Best of Breed with Stanley Masaki's Fuku Masa-Go going Best of Opposite Sex, out of an entry of seventy-five under judge Masaru Matsuda at the **AKIHO Los Angeles Branch** show.

The then-active Eastern Akita Club held a Specialty Match in 1972. Once more, Best of Breed was Sakura's Bushi, CD, and Best of Opposite Sex, O'Shea Princess Hana-Go, owned by Lil O'Shea and L. Wright. East Coast breeder Lil O'Shea provided much of the fine original breeding stock for some of today's kennels. She was dedicated to the Akita.

Recognition came in 1973 and with it the task of providing Sanctioned Matches that would lead to Licensed Specialties.

SPECIALTIES SINCE AKC RECOGNITION

After fulfilling the requirements set forth by the American Kennel Club (holding Sanctioned A and B Matches) so that the Parent Club knew what procedures to follow, the very first Akita Club of America National Specialty show was held. In accordance with AKC regulations, the next few years Specialties would be held in conjunction with AKC licensed all-breed shows.

The first National Specialty was held in Northridge, California, at the San Fernando Kennel Club fixture. Starting time was 8:00 A.M. on a hot, muggy October 17, 1976. The memory has not yet dimmed. The Akitas milled around in an open-sided, cement-bottomed cattle show barn at the old Devonshire fairgrounds. This area has since been elevated to student housing for California State University of Northridge. By high noon not a breath of air moved; dogs and handlers alike showed excitement and strain.

C. L. Savage judged the Sweepstakes. Out of an entry of thirty-six, he chose Gaylee's Fonzi No Kosetsu for his winning dog.

Dale McMackin was the club's choice as judge for the regular breed classes. He could not fulfill his assignment and Council Parker took his place.

The Best of Breed winner of this first and historic Specialty was Ch. Gaylee's O'Kaminaga, owned and handled by Leon Nogue. This impressive dog went on to capture a Group second placement in the all-breed competition later that day.

Cleveland, Ohio, was the next Specialty on December 12, 1976. The location and the weather, and the fact that this Specialty was too close to the first one, prevented a prime entry. There were only twenty class Akitas entered, with Kitty Drury judging. Richard Woods had a Sweepstakes entry of a mere five. Mrs. Drury chose Fio Kita Bear Ali for her Best of Breed with D'Larus Call of the Wild winning the Sweeps.

Northhampton, Massachusetts, on July 14, 1977, brought Carolyn D. Thomas out to judge the next National. Best of Breed went to Ch. Gin-Gin Haiyaku-Go of Sakusaku, with Best of Opposite Sex going to White Paws-Inu-Imero. Robert Thomas judged Sweeps and placed Indian Hy's Grizzly Bear in the lead position.

The Specialty in 1978 was a huge success. Hosted by the Great Lakes Akita Club, it was held on November 11 in Griffith, Indiana. Dale McMackin finally got the chance to do an Akita Specialty and was presented with an entry of 111 including 29 in the Specials Class. Best of Breed went to Ch. Nan Chao's Samurai No Chenko and Best of Opposite Sex to Ch. Big A's Stormy of Jobe. Winners Dog for five points was the Best in Sweepstakes winner Frakari's Date Tensha Dibotsu. Kyoto's Kibu No Kobi was Winners Bitch.

Sweepstakes was judged by Joan Linderman. The judging started promptly at 8:00 A.M. with forty-five Akitas ranging from six to eighteen months of age. Out of the forty-five, Best in Sweepstakes went to Frakari's Date Tensha Dibotsu.

The two judges saw eye-to-eye in their placements, and the judging was consistent for both regular breed classes and Sweepstakes.

The Santa Clara County Fairgrounds, San Jose, California, was the setting for the next Specialty, September 9, 1979. Thelma Brown judged the breed competition. Puppy Sweepstakes were adjudicated by Jim Hohe. The ring was situated outside, and although

Ch. GIN-GIN HAIYAKU-GO OF SAKUSAKU.   *Photo by Joan Ludwig.*

it got exceedingly warm as the day wore on, it was a spacious ring, well set up and comfortable for both dogs and spectators.

Mrs. Brown drew an entry of 133 including 31 Specials. Her Best of Breed was Ch. Gaylee's O'Kaminaga from the Veteran Dog Class. Bred by C. and D. Clifford and owned by L. Nogue, this stylish male, who was to be eight years old on December 1, performed well for his second Specialty win. Best of Opposite Sex was Ch. Jo-San's Seibo No Kosetsu, owned by C. Foti and J. Batausa. Best in Sweepstakes was Edo's Saitochi No Jo-San.

In the years between 1980 and 1990, the Parent Club had

Ch. TOSHIRO'S ROM. "Toshi" (*left*) won the Brood Bitch class at the 1986 National, handled by Sylvia Thomas and owned by Wally and Betty Yelverton, longtime Akita supporters.

earned the right to put on independent Specialties and regional Specialties held by affiliated clubs. Because of the huge increase in entries and added classes, Specialties now had more judges, with shows sometimes lasting more than one day.

Following are the primary results of the Akita Club of America Specialties:

1980 Houston, Texas
BOB—Big A's Stormy of Jobe
BOS—Okii Yubi's Mr. Man
1981 Pomona, California
BOB—Ch. Matsukaze's Holly Go Litely
BOS—Ch. Satori's Asahi-Go
1982 Ravenna, Ohio
BOB—Ch. Kenjiko Royal Tenji
BOS—Ch. Matsukaze's Holly Go Litely
1983 New Lenox, Illinois
BOB—Ch. Kenjiko Royal Tenji
BOS—Ch. O'BJ Kye Kye-Go of E Oka
1984 Portland, Oregon
BOB—Ch. Asahi Yama No Hanashi
BOS—Ch. Jo-San's Seibo No Kosetsu

Ch. HOT'S MO'S BARNABY JONES, ROM. Sire: Ch. Hot's Melvin O; Dam: Ch. Frerose's Annie Till. Owned by John D'Alessio, this very attractive dog achieved his ROM status with 38 champions; won Best of Breed at the 1986 National and four Regionals, and produced three Best in Show offspring.

1985 St. Petersburg, Florida
BOB—Ch. HOT's Mo's Barnaby Jones
BOS—Ch. Toshiro's
1986 Del Mar, California
BOB—Ch. Brook-Staten Deja Vu
BOS—Ch. Crown Royal's Akai O Kashi, CD
1987 Wallingford, Connecticut
BOB—Ch. Tamarlane's Veni Vidi Vici
BOS—Ch. Frakari's Date Tensha Pot Luck
1988 Denver, Colorado
BOB—Ch. Brook-Staten's Maxwell Smart
BOB—Ch. Kuroi Kao Dallas Alice
1989 San Rafael, California
BOB—Ch. Sho-Go's Rambo
BOS—Ch. Apogee's Green With Envy

212

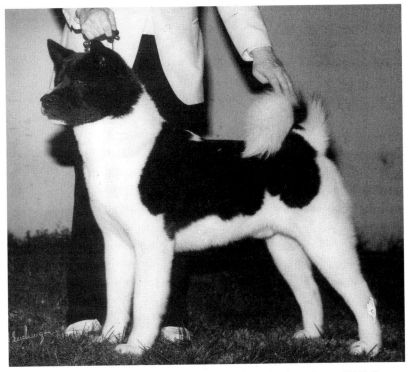

Ch. BROOK-STATEN DEJA-VU. Sire: Ch. Hot's Mo's Barnaby Jones, ROM; Dam: Ch. Hot's Messiah'D Krisje. Bred by John D'Alessio and owned by J. D'Alessio and C. Wiltshire. Deja-Vu was Best of Breed at the 1986 National.

1990 Knoxville, Tennessee
      BOB—Ch. Tobe's Return of the Jedi
      BOS—Ch. Panmark's Musicmaker of Seisan
1991 Ontario, California
      BOB—Ch. Northstar's Mad Maxx
      BOS—AKC award rescinded
1992 Houston, Texas
      BOB—Ch. Allure Island's Shogun
      BOS—Ch. Frakari's Martha Washington
1993 Marlboro, Massachusetts
      BOB—Ch. Tobe's Return of the Jedai
      BOS—Ch. Do-T-Do Kliquot of Akiko

Ch. BROOK-STATEN MAXWELL SMART. Sire: Ch. Hot's Mo's Barnaby Jones, ROM; Ch. Kato's Itsi Bitsi Brenda. Owned by John D'Alessio and handled by Kathy Mines. Maxwell Smart was Best of Breed at the 1988 National.

By consulting the ROM lists and pedigrees and reviewing the above National Specialty winners, you can determine how many Akitas went on to make other major contributions to breed history.

SPECIALTY CONTRIBUTIONS

A Specialty is something more than just a time for the renewal of old friendships. It is a time when the spectator (the armchair judge on the outside of the ring) has the best chance to look long and hard at how certain lines are developing, and to take note of how the youngsters that were seen six months or a year ago are developing.

Continuity of quality, without widely divergent types, is a good indication that a line is fairly consistent. You can see that

Ch. NORTH STAR'S MAD MAXX. Sire: Ch. O'BJ's Zack the Spotted Bear, ROM. Dam: Ch. Kuroi Kao Dallas Alice, ROM. Maxx is owned by S. and F. Thomas and C. and M. Schipper, and handled by Bruce Schultz. Maxx was the 1991 National winner.

Ch. KYUKAZAN'S TIGER BLOSSOM. Best in Sweeps, 1986 National under judge Janet Voss. Owned/handled by Carol Parker.

some lines mature more slowly than others, and whether or not you feel the older dogs in these lines hold up better over the years. If several generations are present, you can try to trace certain characteristics of type. The serious breeder wants to see improvement in some areas in each succeeding generation.

That is the purpose of it all, not just producing litter after litter to have pups for sale. Aside from the major structural areas of concern (hips, shoulders, etc.), there is much to be seen. Is eye color and shape good? Does it improve? What about the size, shape and set of the ears; are they nicely hooded or splayed open like a radar saucer? Are the feet and toes tight and compact? Be sure to check for relative length of bone in the toes. What about the length

216

and arch of the neck, set and curl of the tail, depth of color, quality of coat and all the rest? Type must be stressed along with soundness, or as the saying goes, "Why not just bring the X-ray into the ring?"

Use your Specialties as a learning experience and a living pedigree.

Sixth Annual Jonan Branch AKIKYO Show. KUMA-GO BAHI, the white dog in right foreground was owned and shown by George Hall, who lived in Japan, where he had established his kennel. Some of the Bahi dogs were in the early pedigrees of our U.S. Akitas, i.e., Yukihime-Go Bahi and Shiro Bohe-Go Bahi.

15

The Show Ring in Japan and America

JAPAN

Nipponken Hozonkai (NIPPO) held its first dog show on November 6, 1932, and one every year following until 1942. Only *native Japanese* dogs were shown. Few Akitas were represented at most of these events.

Akitainu Kyokai (AKIKYO) was organized in Tokyo in October 1948. The first Akikyo show was held the following year in conjunction with the thirteenth memorial services for the faithful Akita dog Hachiko.

In the beginning it appears AKIKYO had some association with AKIHO. According to old records, AKIHO recognized the establishment of the Akitainu Kyokai in Tokyo in 1949. It also shows that Mr. Katsusuke Ishihara, who was an important figure from the beginning of AKIKYO, was also an AKIHO judge who judged the Fifteenth AKIHO Headquarters shows. One is not sure for what reason AKIKYO became separated from AKIHO, but it seems to have occurred around April 1955 when AKIKYO incorporated.

Since AKIKYO was established rather late, after NIPPO and AKIHO, its main sphere of influence in the beginning was in the Kanto Region, with Tokyo as the center. Later, branches were established in the Tohoku, Tokai and Tozai regions. More recently they have expanded to Chugoku, Shikoku and parts of Kyushu. However, the branches seem to be more heavily concentrated in the Kanto Region, with a few branches scattered rather sparsely in other regions. Therefore, fewer dog shows are held in AKIKYO.

The famed AKIHO organization, registering body for Akitas only, held a show after World War II in November 9, 1947. Although shows might have been given during the war, this was considered the eleventh. Sadly, records are not available.

There are three types of AKIHO shows in Japan, in order, as follows:

1. Branch Shows—May have more than 300 single entries.
2. Regional Shows—Five or six branches may put on an area regional show. However, only the exceptional branch show winners are eligible for a regional show.
3. Headquarters Shows—Held spring and fall with only the top dogs from the regional shows allowed to enter. Entry can run upwards of 300 dogs.

Opening show ceremonies are both elaborate and solemn. Club and Japanese colors are displayed. Club members serve as helpers and wear colorful club jackets. Trophy tables are laden with exquisite scrolls and silver. Judges are conservatively but elegantly dressed and wear traditional red and white rosettes. Official photographers wear club armbands.

Presentation

Each Japanese Akita is presented beautifully and in *full coat only*. Dogs and bitches are flawlessly groomed. They wear magnificent double collars: a round leather with a gold or silver choke chain attached. A six-foot braided silk lead, in gold or red, completes the

Adult Akita dog in full show regalia. Note that collar and chest piece are special equipment.

picture. Dogs and equipment are an expensive investment. Top Akitas have been sold in the $25,000 and up range.

Procedure and Protocol

There is a head official table where persons of importance are seated. Besides the judges, officials and honored guests, government dignitaries frequently appear. Before judging, the judges are introduced. Speeches of welcome follow.

The showgrounds are one huge circle inside which are several white-circled rings approximately 12 feet in diameter. Small silver bowls are placed at the edges for judges to wash hands after their "touch" examinations of each dog.

In addition to the Chief or Head Judge, there is a panel of judges whose number depends on the total entry in show. Each judge can only go over thirty individual dogs at one show. This is what is called a "Specialist Judge." That is one who judges only Akitas, has had from ten to twenty years experience with the breed

221

A typical young Japanese show Akita.

and has apprenticed under older, more knowledgeable judges for many, many years. In most cases, this person is or has been a breeder of Akitas.

The show begins with the *Yoken Class*, the six-to-ten-month-old dogs and bitches. Dogs are situated at one end of the ring complex, bitches at another. The judges do a written critique on each entry. Except for checking for black spots on the tongue, counting teeth to ascertain correct bite and a testicle check on males, *they do not handle the dog. It is primarily a visual exam.* The Akitas are presented individually in a natural stance. The handlers stand

222

秋 保 審 査 表　　　第　　　回　　　展

| 犬 NAME OF DOG | | 犬 号 | KENNEL | 毛 COLOR | 体 HEIGHT |
| 名 | | 舎 | | 色 | 高 |

登 録 番 号 REG. NO.　　　号 DATE　年　月　日　AGE　蔵　月

| 父 SIRE | 号 | 出 NAME OF OWNER |
| 母 DAM | 号 | 陳 者 |

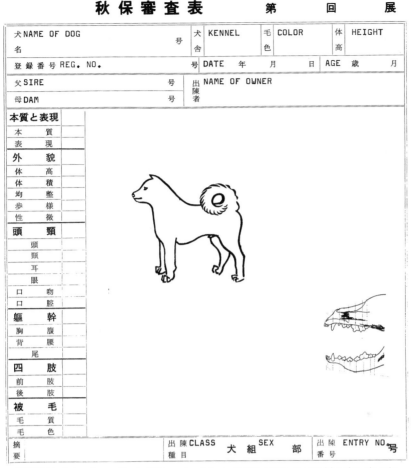

本質と表現	
本	質
表	現
外	**貌**
体	高
体	積
均	整
歩	様
性	徴
頭	**頸**
頭	
頸	
耳	
眼	
口	吻
口	腔
軀	**幹**
胸	腹
背	腰
尾	
四	**肢**
前	肢
後	肢
被	**毛**
毛	質
毛	色

摘要

出 陳 CLASS 種 目　　　犬　組　SEX　部　出 陳 ENTRY NO. 番 号　　号

AKIHO judging form. Each Akita entry has a sheet which is used by the show's judges. The judges, in turn, make the awards based on their agreement of the winning animals.

well behind or to the side of their charges and are not permitted to position them. Baiting with food is not allowed.

When judging of the Yoken is completed, the *Wakainu*, or 10 to 18 Month Class, is judged, followed by the *Soken*, or 18 to 30 Month Class, and the *Seiken*, or 30 Month and Over Class. In all of these classes the dogs are judged as to how well they adhere to the Standard, *not* whether one dog is better than the other.

TOCHIKUMO-GO. Mr. Mitsuru's Okabayashi's Tokuyu award at the 75th Head-quarters show in Odate City.

In the afternoon, the equivalent of our American Group judging is held. Placements are made from one through fifteen in each class. It is conceivable to have fifty or more dogs in a class.

The grading system is as follows:

Tokuyu—Superior (awarded to Senior Dogs and Bitches only)
Yusho—Excellent

Junyu—Good

Nintei—Satisfactory

Shikkau—Disqualification (Unacceptable at that time)

The MEIYOSHO, the highest award that can be attained by an Akita in Japan, is awarded to dogs and bitches at Headquarters-sponsored shows. Only dogs and bitches who have achieved the Tokuyu rating qualify. These dogs are considered to have extra-special qualities. "A Meiyosho winner," according to Mr. Zenzo Watanabe, one of the three most experienced judges of AKIHO, "is not merely the top winning dog of a particular Headquarters show. As the Akita is judged according to an absolute Standard, a given show may produce a Meiyosho winner, may not produce a winner or may produce more than one winner. Therefore, these winners may be considered the Grand Champions of AKIHO shows."

A Meiyosho winner can never compete again, only be exhibited.

Though AKIHO judging procedure is different, the all-breed Japan Kennel Club shows are judged much like we do our all-breed events.

The Japan Kennel Club

The JKC is the latest of international registering bodies to be recognized by the AKC, and is of great concern now to the Akita Club of America. The all-breed JKC shows are judged much as we do in our all-breed events in the United States.

IN AMERICA

All dog shows where championship points are awarded, whether all-breed or Specialty, are held under the rules and regulations of the American Kennel Club, whose responsibility it is to approve judges, register purebred dogs and keep records of every dog's points.

Strictly speaking, any purebred Akita eligible for registration with the AKC can compete at licensed dog shows. He or she must

SANMARK SUNFIRE OF NORTHLAND, a lovely red bitch whelped 12/3/89, being shown at four months of age. Handled by owner, Loren Egland, and judged by Carol Parker, Sunfire is a striking example of how many recently bred American Akitas resemble their Japanese counterparts.

be at least six months old and cannot have one of the disqualifying faults, as noted in the Standard for the breed. Lame or altered dogs may not be shown.

Before stepping into a show ring, a dog should be accustomed to crowds, a leash and handling, and be well groomed. Unlike counterparts in Japan, the Akita in America is shown with a simple choke chain and leather show lead, and is often hand-stacked and baited with food.

Shows where championship points are awarded are either benched or unbenched. At a benched show, dogs must remain in partitioned stalls for all or part of the day. They are secured by a bench chain or a crate. At an unbenched show, they may be taken home after their class has been judged, provided they are not needed for Group judging.

Sometimes a club holds a Sanctioned Match Show under a plan designated as ''Plan B'' or ''Plan A'' by AKC. No championship points are awarded at these fixtures. Many ''fun matches'' are given by clubs or organizations that are not sanctioned by AKC. All Matches are important training grounds for puppies and dogs who will later compete at a point show.

How Dogs Are Judged

The judge is guided by the Standard of perfection for each breed when making selections. This Standard describes what is considered a perfect specimen of the breed, and often the relative importance of each detail. The Standard also lists definite faults that are to be discouraged or penalized in the breed.

Judges must study each dog carefully, with their hands as well as their eyes, when the dog is in motion as well as standing. The texture of the coat is checked, as is firmness of muscle and bone and soundness of teeth. The way a dog moves is important, not only for beauty in motion, but as a test of body structure.

There are a number of things the handler can do to show a dog to best advantage, and the dog with a lively, intelligent personality and sense of showmanship often has an advantage. But the basis of judging in the show ring is the physical beauty and structural soundness of the dog. The judge compares the dogs in each class

227

TETSURYU TAESHITA KENSHA. Sire: Kita No Unryu of Sasahara Kensha; Dam: Saki of Fukuoko Shirayukiso. Breeder: Susumu Kuro Kawn. Japanese import, 1992. Owned by Bobrow, Parker, Kam, Sakayeda.

and makes the awards to those that best meet the requirements of the Standard.

With the advent of imports once again being allowed into the United States from Japan, it is *inevitable* that some changes will be made in breed type. This will take place slowly and painlessly for the most part.

The Point System

Dogs get points toward a championship and qualify for the top awards as follows:

Regular Classes

All dogs competing for championship points are entered in one of the regular classes for their breed and sex. The classes for dogs and classes for bitches are:

228

PUPPY: For dogs under one year. May be divided 6 to 9 and 9 to 12 months. May not be champions.

12 to 18 MONTH: For dogs at least 12 months and under 18 months as of date of show.

NOVICE: For dogs not having won three firsts in Novice, none in other classes, except puppy, nor any championship points.

BRED BY EXHIBITOR: For dogs not champions, owned wholly or partly by breeder; shown by one of the breeders of record, or a member of the breeder's immediate family.

AMERICAN-BRED: For all dogs, except champions, born in the United States, resulting from a mating that took place in the U.S.

OPEN: For any dog.

HACHIME OF ONISHI KENSHA. Sire: Genpei of Kumamoto Ishimura Kensha; Dam: Sakuraichimime of Kitakyushu Kensha. This fine five-year-old red import went Winner's Bitch at the 1992 National. Bred by the noted Kiyomi Onishi, "Aki" is owned by F. and A. Sakayeda, C. Parker, C. Kam.

WINNERS DOG: The first-place winner of each class (which has not been beaten in any other class) competes for Winners Dog. He receives a purple ribbon and points proportionate to the number of males present.

RESERVE WINNERS DOG: The second-place dog having been defeated only by the dog chosen Winners Dog, competes with the dogs remaining in the ring (unless he has already been defeated by one of them) for Reserve Winners. The Reserve Winners Dog receives a purple-and-white ribbon, and moves up to Winners if the Winners Dog is for any reason disqualified.

WINNERS BITCH AND RESERVE WINNERS BITCH: Same procedure followed as that for Winners Dog and Reserve Winners Dog.

BEST OF WINNERS: If the Winners Dog or Winners Bitch is awarded Best of Breed, it automatically is awarded Best of Winners; otherwise, the Winners Dog and Winners Bitch are judged together for Best of Winners. In addition to the blue-and-white ribbon, the Best of Winners may receive additional points if the winner of the opposite sex had an entry qualifying for higher points.

BEST OF BREED: The Winners Dog and Winners Bitch compete for Best of Breed with any champions entered for Best of Breed along with winners of single entry nonregular classes such as Veteran or Field Dog. If BOB or BOS is either Winners Dog or Winners Bitch, then any champions defeated are also counted toward the scale of points awarded. The winner receives a purple-and-gold ribbon.

Champions entered in the BOB class are dogs and bitches that have acquired sufficient points in previous competition. If there are no champions entered, the Best of Winners is automatically Best of Breed. The other dog or bitch competing for Best of Winners is Best of Opposite Sex.

BEST OF OPPOSITE SEX: Following selection of Best of Breed and Best of Winners, all individuals of the sex opposite to BOB remain in the ring. The Winners Dog or Winners Bitch, whichever is also of the sex opposite to Best of Breed, is judged in this class. From this group, Best of Opposite Sex is chosen. A red-and-white ribbon is awarded to the Best of Opposite Sex to Best of Breed.

THE GROUP: The Akita competes in the Working Group. The blue rosette for first in Group is given to the winner among all Best of Breed dogs competing in that particular group. Red, yellow and white rosettes are also given to the second, third and fourth place winners in Group.

BEST IN SHOW: The seven Group winners are judged for the top award Best in Show. A rosette colored red, white and blue is given.

Note: Four ribbons are awarded in each class—blue for first, red for second, yellow for third and white for fourth, unless the judge chooses to withhold a ribbon(s) for lack of merit. Champions may compete in Open classes, but are usually entered for Best of Breed only, as they do not need the championship points awarded to Winners Dog and Winners Bitch. To become a champion, a dog or bitch must win a total of fifteen points under at least three judges. Within that, a dog must win a minimum of three points in each of two shows under different judges.

A FIRST—AND A PATH TO THE FUTURE

It is conceivable that in the future the Akita will be a prominent member of the First in Group/Best in Show elite with great regularity. We look forward to the day when the breed will take a backseat to no other.

That path was begun in 1977 by a special dog who earned a special win—Brownie.

Brownie's Story

His name was Ch. Wanchan's Akagumo and he was bred by Dr. Peter Lagus. At first he made his home with Linda Goldsby Lewis but was returned to his breeder while still a young dog.

Pete felt that show potential was there and proceeded to groom the youngster for the ring. As is the case with most slow-maturing Akitas, Brownie was six years old before he had reached his full potential. But the time was right for him, and with his owner's faith and conditioning and the help of his co-owner, Carol Foti, he was campaigned. On June 5, 1977, at the San Joaquin Kennel Club fixture, in Stockton, California, Judge Anna Katherine Nicholas gave Brownie and Carol the nod. Brownie had the honor of becoming the first Akita in the United States to go Best in Show.

In his show career, he placed first in the Working Group five times with a total of sixteen Group placements. To quote his owner, "He loved people, loved to perform, loved the applause." Brownie sired nine champions. Two of these, Ch. Va-Guas The Mean Machine and Ch. Toyo no Charlie Brown were awarded the ROM.

Brownie died of a massive coronary at home in the family room where he lived among the kennelmates and humans who had shared his great moments.

16

The Register of Merit

THE REGISTER OF MERIT for Akitas was introduced in 1980, when the Akita Club of America made the point system official. The efforts of the Tampa Bay Akita Club, member of the Akita Club of America and Susan Oswald helped pull the project together.

The first official list of ROM dogs and bitches contained the names of thirteen stud dogs and twenty-seven bitches.

In order for a sire to become eligible for the ROM designation, he must have produced at least ten champion offspring; the bitch, at least five.

The list of ROM sires and dams that follows is current through mid-1994 and was compiled by the Akita Club of America Registry of Merit committee, using the AKC *Gazette* as their guide.

It must be pointed out that for this day and age, where the breed is growing in size and peaking in popularity, the present-day system may become outdated.

In order to improve the system, the Parent Club must take a close look at the ROM systems used by other breed organizations. One in particular was patterned after the highly successful ROM formulated by the American Hereford Association where a point system is used.

Ch. TOSHIRO'S, ROM. Sire: Ch. Triple K Tomo-Go, ROM; Dam: Koinu. "Toshi," born 1/31/77, and owned by Walter (Wally) and Betty Yelverton.

ROM SIRES

Akiko's Foxy Ted, Ch. (3/94)
Akita Tani's Daimyo, Ch. (12/81)
    "   "   Kuro Chikara (4/78)
    "   "   Tatsumaki (2/78)
Allure Island's Shogun, Ch. (1/92)
Cee Jay's Chumley P. Linderman, Ch. (11/81)
Crown Royal's American Dream Boy, Ch. (12/92)
    "   "   Slugo-Go, Ch. (4/89)

Ch. CEE-JAY'S CHUMLEY P. LINDERMAN, ROM. Sire: Ch. Gin-Gin Haiyaku-Go of Sakusaku, ROM; Dam: Akijikan's Aki. Owned by Ben and Ann Tomazewski.

Frakari's Date Tensha Dibotsu, Ch. (12/86)
Fu-Ki's Hideki Tojo, Ch. (9/89)
Fukumoto's Ashibaya Kuma, Ch. (3/77)
Gaylee's O'Kaminaga, Ch. (2/82)
Gin-Gin's Haiyaku-Go of Sakusaku, Ch. (9/76)
Goshen's Chariots O'Fire, Ch. (1/92)
Gr. River's Galloping Gourmet, Ch. (9/87)
HOT's I Have Arrived, Ch. (4/83)
   "   Melvin O, Ch. (2/88)
   "   Mo's Barnaby Jones, Ch. (2/87)
   "   Van Scoten Jones, Ch. (6/82)
Bar B J's Brown Bomber, Ch. (9/86)
Jag's Hercules, Ch. (6/87)

Am/Can Ch. KAKWA'S ORCA, ROM. Sire: Am/Can Ch. Shuso Saki Tumi of Okii Yubi; Dam: Am/Berm/Can Ch. Langan's Amateratsu O-Mi-Kami. Bred by Andy Russell, owned by B. J. and Bill Andrews.

Jakura's Pharfossa Michael, Ch. (6/83)

Kakwa's Orca, Ch. (5/84)

Kelly's Ray Gin Bull of Frerose, CD, Ch. (11/89)

Kenjiko Royal Tenji, Ch. (11/78)

Ketket's Hug-A-Tuck of Khalea, Ch. (7/93)

Kim Sai's Royal Jakara Kuma, Ch. (2/86)

Kin Hozan's Toklat, CD, Ch. (9/83)

Kin Ko, Ch. (2/81)

Komu Inu Bronze Bruin, Ch. (1/93)

Krug's Yoshinori, Ch. (9/83)

Mikado No Kin Hozan (3/80)

Ch. OKII YUBI'S SACHMO OF MAKOTO, ROM. Bred by Robert Campbell and owned and shown by Barbara (B. J.) Andrews, Sachmo sired 49 litters and produced 102 champions.

Mike Truax's Royal Tikara Pal, Ch. (11/87)

Mokusei's Zeus of Daitan-Ni, Ch. (1/92)

Nami's Shokko of Oka., CD, Ch. (11/93)

Nan Chao's Samurai No Chenko, Ch. (6/84)

Noji's The Count Crown Royal, Ch. (7/91)

O'BJ's Bigson of Sachmo, Ch. (6/84)

O'BJ High N Mighty No Goshen, Ch. (3/86)

    "   King's Ransom, Ch. (6/89)

    "   Zach the Spotted Bear, Ch. (9/91)

Okii Yubi's Mr. Judge, Ch. (2/81)

    "   "   Sachmo of Makoto, Ch. (1/79)

Pharfossa's Jabo West Bay, Ch. (7/87)

    "   Outlaw Josey Wales, Ch. (7/89)

Ch. OKII YUBI'S DRAGON HOUSE KO-GO, ROM. Sire: Yukan No Okii Yubi; Dam: Ko Tori No Okii Yubi. Bred by Bob Campbell, this male produced 15 champions and is owned by B. and B. J. Andrews.

Raiden of Jo-Uba, Ch. (12/88)
Sakusaku's Tom Cat-Go, Ch.
Sho-Go's Joboy Tuff-N-Stuff, Ch. (9/89)
Shori's Daisan Banku Maru, Ch. (8/79)
Taki's Akaguma Sakura, Ch. (12/77)
Tamarlane's Brigadoon, Ch. (12/86)
    "   Khaiber, Ch. (6/89)
    "   Kuma-Yama Khan, Ch. (5/87)
    "   Veni Vedi Vici, Ch. (5/91)
Tamarlane's Willowdeen Aikon, Ch. (2/91)
Tobe's Abrakadabra, Ch. (12/86)
    "   Adam of Genesis, Ch. (8/89)
    "   Return of the Jedi, Ch. (7/91)
Toshiro's Karate Drift, Ch. (12/84)

Ch. TOYO NO CHARLIE BROWN, ROM. Sire: Ch. Wanchan's Akagumo, ROM; Dam: Japanese Grand Ch. Haru Hime, ROM. Bred by D. D. and Barbara Confer; owned and handled by Carol Foti.

Toyo-No Charlie Brown, Ch. (2/82)

Triple K Tomo-Go, Ch. (12/80)

Va-Guas Jamel The Mean Machine, Ch. (12/80)

Windrift's Teddy Bear, Ch. (6/83)

Yokohama's Daitan Okami Go, Ch. (8/86)

Yukan No Okii Yubi

Yuko's Happy Grizzly, Ch. (6/90)

Ch. THE WIDOW-MAKER O'BJ, ROM. Sire: The Real McCoy O'BJ; Dam: Ch. The Same Dame O'BJ, ROM. Bred, owned, handled by B. J. Andrews, this winning male has captured ten Bests in Show.

ROM DAMS

Akemi's Tsukimaru Go, Ch. (11/83)
Akita Tani's Kuro Shuso (2/78)
Alii's Storm Warning, Ch. (12/89)
Bear of Thor's Ninno, Ch. (5/89)
Beastie of Toshiros, Ch. (3/80)
Bighorns Kitai Suru, Ch. (6/90)
Butterworth Bog Sumi Mendo, Ch. (6/81)
Cho-Jo's Sumiko Hime, Ch. (1/86)
Costa Brava's A Touch of Class, Ch. (1/82)
Crown Royal's Akai O'Kashi, CD, Ch. (5/89)

Mex. Ch. SAKUSAKU GOROTSUKI-GO, ROM. Sire: Triple K Hayai Taka; Dam: Ichiban Mitsubachi, CD.

      "   "   Candy Contessa, Ch. (5/93)
      "   "   Toker Too, Ch. (2/92)
Daijobu's Vampirella O'BJ, Ch. (11/87)
Date Tensha's Pot Luck, Ch. (3/89)
Don-D's Dietka of the HOT, Ch. (7/76)
Dragonfire Cressida (7/91)
Echol's Ichi-Ban Tamiko, Ch. (3/80)

Ch. CROWN ROYAL'S TOKER TOO, ROM. Sire: Ch. Kin Hozan's Toklat CD, ROM; Dam: Crown Royal's Intara Sueling. Owners Jerry and Ingrid Linerud.

E Oka's Puttin on the Ritz, Ch. (5/91)
Fio Princess Kira of Kirabran, Ch. (10/80)
Frerose's Annie Til, Ch. (9/86)
    "   Aubrie (3/84)
    "   Betty Jo (6/82)
    "   Char-Dan of the HOT, Ch. (8/83)
    "   Dark Moon of Sho-Go, Ch. (2/88)
    "   Gypsy Rose, Ch. (11/82)
    "   Honey Bear, Ch. (9/87)
    "   Sarah Lei, Ch. (2/82)
Golden Sun's Seawood Wawalwila, Ch. (3/88)

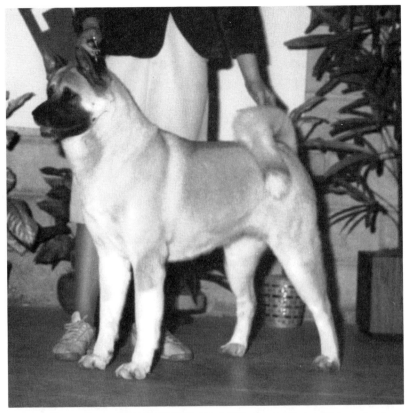

Ch. CROWN ROYAL'S AKAI OKASHI CD, ROM. Group placing bitch owned by Ingrid and Jerry Linerud.

Goshen's Jungle Jenny of Noji, Ch. (7/90)
     "   Kuroi Tar Baby, Ch. (8/90)
     "   Shadowdancer Haikara, Ch. (3/93)
     "   The Silver Lining, Ch. (8/93)
Gr. River's Sunshine On My Mind, Ch. (6/90)
Hara Hime (2/75)
HOT's Kooky Kita (12/81)
Jade Ko Samurai, Ch. (5/81)
JAG's Kami, Ch. (6/83)
Jo-San's Seibo No Kosetsu, Ch. (12/90)
Jube's Aki Tesu's Shokin, Ch. (9/87)
     "   Aki Yuki Shika, Ch. (5/89)

Juho Mariko No Kin Hozan (11/78)
Kajo's Wicked Witch, Ch. (12/86)
Kamoti's Su Zee Bo Mar (2/87)
Karasu Oka No Shiminawa, Ch. (9/90)
Karisma's Another Kind of Cane (1/86)
Keoshe Samurai Lee Down (3/91)
Ketket's Tigger No Nan Chao, Ch. (10/85)
Kimiko of Frerose, Ch. (9/79)
Kimino Kuro Siwo No Pearl (5/90)
Kin Sue's B-B, Ch. (3/93)
Kinouk's Alia (9/87)
    "   Chick-A-Boom, Ch. (7/88)
    "   Kor-I, Ch. (5/80)
    "   Tabitha of Salt Brush, Ch. (2/85)

Ch. JO-SAN'S SEIBO NO KOSETSU, ROM. Breeders, Joe and Sandy Batausa.

Kita Hoshi Kuma of Windrift, Ch. (10/82)
Kofuku No's Shoga Hime (6/78)
Krug's Tenshi Okami, Ch. (1/83)
Kuma Yama's Golden Star, Ch. (8/84)
Kuroi Kao Dallas Alice, Ch. (8/90)
Kuro Panzu Maru No Asagao, Ch. (10/78)
Lenmar's Sachiko (7/91)

Ch. SAKUSAKU'S PERFECT PEARL, ROM. Sire: Ch. Gin-Gin Haiyaku-Go of Sakusaku, ROM; Dam: Sakusaku Gorotsuki-Go, ROM.

SHIMI-KUMA, ROM. Sire: Toryu-Go; Dam: Triple K Yoko. Shimi was bred by Tom and Jeanette Nishioka of Los Angeles.

Lijo's Spirit of Tobe, Ch. (10/79)
Magic Lady Jackalyn, Ch. (1/89)
Masumi's Lady Sunshine, Ch. (1/89)
    ″   Ninja Kara Suteki, Ch. (9/89)
Matsu-Kaze's Chereed Notakali, Ch. (2/79)
    ″   Key Too Kinouk, Ch. (3/80)
    ″   Kuro Ban Kuma, Ch. (8/84)
Maxwell's Kuro Ban Kuma, Ch. (8/84)
    ″   Shadow of Abby, Ch. (3/90)
Me-Tu of To-Zu, Ch. (2/84)
Ms. Matsu-Kaze Loves Company, Ch. (4/80)
N Bar J's Akarri Su of Kajo, Ch. (11/80)
Nishi-Taiyo Joto Fujin, Ch. (8/89)
O'BJ Dame of the Game, Ch. (12/88)
    ″   Georgia Peach, Ch. (5/85)

246

Ch. TORI'S YOI TOY OF CHIHEISEN, ROM. Sire: Am/Can Ch. Kin Hozan's Toklat CD, ROM; Dam: Ch. Amai Shiroi Takara. Born 3/14/82; owned by Sylvia, Frank and Warren Byrd; handled by Betty Littschwager.

"   Kichmo of Kirabran, Ch. (3/86)

"   Kotausha-No of Westwind, Ch. (10/85)

"   Ko-Tausha Tuc, Ch. (7/91)

"   Kye-Kye-Go of E Oka, Ch. (2/89)

"   Michiko of Wri, Ch. (4/86)

"   Nikki No Nikki, Ch. (11/83)

"   One-of-a-Kind, Ch. (12/93)

"   Tarbaby De Alicia (7/87)

Okami's Kori of Krug, Ch. (10/83)

Okii Yubi's Dragonhouse Ko-Go, Ch. (7/81)

Okurimono No O'Yuki, Ch. (6/91)

O'Shea Princess Bara-Go, (10/75)

Parksway Oschi of Willowdeen, Ch. (11/85)

Redman's Orange Colored Sky (7/93)

WINDOM'S ALL THAT JAZZ, ROM. Sire: Krug's Red Kadillac; Dam: Lijo's Jasmine of Windom. This bitch, owned and bred by Ed and Adrienne Israel and Gail Schwartz, produced 14 champions for the breed.

Renegades Fawn Companion (4/85)
Sakura's Chujitsu (5/78)
Sakusaku's Daffodil Lil (11/78)
     "   Gorotsuki-Go (10/75)
     "   Perfect Pearl, Ch. (8/81)
Shimi Kuma (12/74)
Sierra W's Rose of Timbersky, Ch. (1/94)
Sno Storm's Peking Jumbo Jet, Ch. (3/91)
Taigi's Little Hana of Jubes, Ch. (12/86)
Tamarlane's Mi-Magic, Ch. (1/89)

"   Silver Star, Ch. (8/86)

Tane-Matsu-Go (7/82)

Ten No Tengoku (8/79)

The Dame's on Target O'BJ, Ch. (4/90)

The Mad Hatter O'BJ, Ch. (3/90)

The Same Dame O'BJ, Ch. (8/90)

Tora's Michiko O'Ryan, Ch. (3/94)

Tori's Yoi Toi of Chiheisen, Ch. (1/90)

Toshiro's, Ch. (9/86)

Toyo-No Namesu Joo (2/76)

To-Zu's Misty Morning, Ch. (6/88)

Triple K Cho Cho, CD, Ch. (7/77)

Von Glava's Toshimai (2/86)

Windom All That Jazz (11/86)

"   No Yamabuki-Go, Ch. (2/88)

Windrift's Chelsi of Ryan (11/91)

"   Orient Express, Ch. (8/90)

"   Tetsu-Ko of Fu-Ki (11/87)

W. W. Shisiedo Sparkling Star, Ch. (3/94)

Yojo Kuma of Linmin (9/84)

Yuko's Red Red Robin De Alicia (2/88)

In Conclusion

THE RESTORATION of the Akita in Japan and in the United States has captivated the interest of thousands of the breed's devotees.

The changes that have evolved over the past years have taken a brisk, rough breed and created an attractive more sophisticated one for us to enjoy. Not that all of the rough edges have been filed off, mind you. One can still catch glimpses of the rowdy, alert dog filled with the same aggression that the breed was infamous for in its more formative years. The insistence of society that the breed should conform and become a less belligerent canine, and the popularity of the Akita as a show dog has effected a more colorful, handsome and slightly more tractable animal.

It is to be noted, however, that the Akita's rapidly escalating popularity has brought with it problems along with the desirable advancements that have been made.

The Akita Standard is quite explicit in its guidelines for owners, breeders, judges and others who hold the fate of the breed appearance and demeanor in their hands.

We impatiently watch the progress being made. One can only hope that the best is yet to come.

Glossary of Terms

AKA: red

AMERICAN-BRED DOG: a dog whelped in the United States

BREEDER: owner or lessee of a bitch at the time of a breeding

BUCHI: pinto

C.D.: Companion Dog (Novice Obedience)

C.D.X.: Companion Dog Excellent (Open Obedience)

CHAMPION OF RECORD: any dog which has won 15 total points under American Kennel Club rules and regulations, including two wins of 3 points or more, under different judges

GOMA: sesame

H.S.I.T.: Highest Score in Trial (Obedience)

HEIGHT IN SHOW RING: judge shall have the authority to make a determination as to whether any dog measures within the specified limits of the standard

HOHO-BOKE: cheeks fading from red to white

JUNRYU: good

KUMA: bear

KURO: black

LAME: impairment of the function of locomotion, regardless of how slight or severe

LIVER: deep reddish-brown color

MATAGI: hunter

MATAGI INU: hunting dog

MEIJI PERIOD: 1866–1912

MEIYOSHI: highest award that can be obtained by an Akita at an AKIHO-headquarters-sponsored show

MESU: female dog

MOKU: long coat

NATURAL: not artificial; in the Akita pertaining to alteration of color or coat

NINTEI: satisfactory

ODATE DOGS: early name given to the Akita dogs' predecessors based on the name of a Japanese province

OVERSHOT: the incisors of the *upper* jaw projecting beyond the incisors of the lower jaw, thus creating a space

PREMIUM LISTS: entry forms and other information for dog shows are contained in these mailings

RUFF: thick, longer hair growth around neck

SEIKEN: 30 months and older

SHIBUSA/SOBOKU: simplicity without adornment

SHIKKAKU: disqualified

SHIRO: white

SHOWA PERIOD: 1926–1941

SICKLE TAIL: carried up in a semicircle

SOKEN: 18–30 month old dog class

STEWARDS: provided to assist judges and to act on a judge's instructions for show ring management

T.D.: Tracking Dog

T.D.X.: Tracking Dog Excellent

TAISHO PERIOD: 1912–1926

TOKUYU: superior

TORA: tiger striped or brindle

U.D.: Utility Dog (Utility Obedience)

U.D.T.: Utility Dog Tracker

U.D.T.X.: Utility Dog Tracker Excellent
UNDERSHOT: the incisors of the *lower* jaw projecting beyond the incisors of the upper jaw when the mouth is closed
WAKAINU: 10–18 month old puppies
YOKEN CLASS: 6–10 month old puppies
YUSHO: excellent

Bibliography of Akita-Related Sources

Akita Newsletter
Akita Kennel Club of America Newsletter
Akita Dog Association of America Breeders Bulletin
Akita Breeders Association Breeders Bulletin
Akita Club of America Newsletter
American Akita Breeders Akita News
The Digest of the Akita Dog Society News
Nisei Week Reports
The Aiken Journal
Insight Documents
The Akita—A Guide
"All About a Dog Show"—Gaines Dog Research Center
Dog World Magazine
State of California Corporation Records Department
Akitainu Hozonkai (AKIHO) Los Angeles Branch
Private letters and papers from the collections of Camille Kam Wong, Marge Rutherford, Linda J. Bruhn, Walter Imai, Margaret Bryant and Ann Diener
Writings of Mr. Naoto Kijiwara, using the translations of Walter Imai
The studies of Dr. Tokiio Kaburagi
The writings of Mr. Hirokichi Sato

Akitainu Tokuhon (*Akita Dog Textbook*) by M. Kiyono.

Mating and Whelping Akita Manual (with some updated material veterinary-approved March 1993) by Joan Linderman, Elizabeth Thayer and Margaret Bryant, as used by the Akita Club of America.

About the Authors

Joan M. Linderman has owned, shown and bred some of the top Akitas in the United States for thirty years, including the first American, Mexican and Canadian international champion of the breed. Her kennel name, Sakusaku, appears on many of the Akita breed's top producers, winners of the coveted Register of Merit award of the Akita Club of America. Ms. Linderman has served the Akita Club of America as president. She was also a member and director of the American Akita Breeders, Inc. A contributing member of *The Akita Review*, she was co-author of the breeding and whelping manual entitled *The Akita—A Guide* and was a co-editor of *The Akita News*.

Ms. Linderman has judged Akitas at numerous all-Akita matches and Specialty show sweepstakes. She was also a recipient of the Gaines Medal for Good Sportsmanship.

In addition, Joan has traveled extensively in Japan and the United States tracking down information on the breed. This has resulted in one of the most extensive collections of breed documentation in America today.

Virginia Funk is an award-winning professional writer and was an AKC-approved judge of German Shepherd Dogs, Belgian Sheepdogs, Belgian Tervuren and Junior Showmanship. She has recently retired from judging.

A selection of writings from her self-syndicated column "Over 50 and Loving It" received the award for Best Column from the Dog Writers Association of America. Previous to that, her column "Leash and Collar" had received a similar award from DWAA. She has also written articles for *Dog Fancy, Popular Dogs, People on Parade* and *Dog Lovers Digest*. Virginia Funk has been a beauty editor for *Senior Life Magazine* and a newspaper columnist for many years. She was also a regular contributor to *Modern Maturity* magazine. In addition to her kennel club activities, Virginia is on the board of directors of Guide Dogs of America.